NOSTRADAMUS
THE MILLENNIUM AND BEYOND

NOSTRADAMUS
THE MILLENNIUM & BEYOND
THE PROPHECIES TO 2016

PETER LORIE

Astrological Consultant, DR. LIZ GREENE

SIMON & SCHUSTER
NEW YORK · LONDON · TORONTO · SYDNEY · TOKOYO · SINGAPORE

SIMON & SCHUSTER

Simon & Schuster Building
Rockefeller Center
1230 Avenue of the Americas
New York, NY 10020

A LABYRINTH BOOK

Copyright © 1993 Labyrinth
Text copyright © 1993 Peter Lorie
Astrological interpretations copyright © 1993 Dr. Liz Greene
Original Illustrations copyright © 1993 Labyrinth
All rights reserved including the right of reproduction in whole or in part in any form
SIMON & SCHUSTER and colophon are registered trademarks of Simon & Schuster Inc.

Design by Moonrunner and Sandipa
Typesetting & Computer Graphics by A. J. Kolpa
Printed by Singapore National Printers Limited, Singapore

1 0 9 8 7 6 5 4 3 2 1

Lorie, Peter
        Nostradamus : the millennium and beyond / Peter Lorie; astrological consultant,
Dr. Liz Greene
                p. cm.
        Includes bibliographical references and index.
        ISBN 0-671-79698-4
        1. Nostradamus, 1503 – 1566. Prophéties. 2 Prophecies (Occultism) 3. Predictive
astrology. 4. Twenty-first century – Forecasting,
I. Greene, Liz. II. Title.
BF1815. N8L58 1993
133.3--dc20   92-43628
                                                                CIP

Annotated Contents

Astrological preface

CAPRICORN

Opposite *~ the "science" of the heavens throughout history was always preceded by fantasy. Mythology and very often beautifully drafted cartography, were brought together to represent the Earth and the skies that surround it. The chart opposite, entitled "The Northern Hemisphere and its Heavens" was first published in Andreas Cellarius's "Atlas Coelestis seu Harmonia Macrocosmica" in 1660 and provides one of the best examples of celestial cartography following the Copernican revolution, containing maps of the Ptolemaic universe, using data compiled by various astronomers with the help of Galileo's telescope. Astronomy and astrology were thus one and the same.*

ROPHECY IS AT THE BEST OF TIMES a chancy business – whether undertaken by a 20th century economist or a 16th century astrologer/clairvoyant. Polls that predict the outcome of a presidential or parliamentary election are as liable to error as the apparently impenetrable out-pourings of a Delphic oracle. But, despite its strangeness and allusiveness, prophetic vision has an ancient and honorable lineage. It was prophecy, after all – visionary and astrological – that predicted the birth of Christ. Such is the power and fascination of prophecy that we keep on trying, not only to find out who will be the next national leader, but, whether Nostradamus really did predict Hitler, AIDS, and the end of the world.

We understand very little about the dynamics of prophecy. Some prophets seem to base their assessments of the future on an intuitive syn-thesis of available facts and known trends. Some are apparently visited unwillingly by visions that, for a time at least, seem to reflect a kind of madness. Some foresee the future in dreams. Some are active practi-tioners of what we are pleased to call magic – a series of psychological techniques, primarily ritualistic, that open the floodgates to the uncon-scious psyche. Still others have availed themselves, throughout history, of what are known as the mantic arts – divination through the flight of birds, the casting of runes, the throwing of coins or yarrow stalks, the laying out of cards, or the patterns of the Sun, Moon, and planets as they move through the zodiacal signs. All of these methods of divining the patterns of the future are based on a principle called synchronicity. Put succinctly, the interconnected organism that is life is reflected at any given moment by its component parts, that embody on some level the meaning and qualities of the moment.

Global prophecy such as that offered by Nostradamus depends upon a capacity to "step out of one's own skin" and achieve an impersonal or

7

transpersonal view of the hidden movements and patterns at work in the collective psyche. Vision of this kind is, however, unreliable in interpretation. However true the symbolic images may be, the level on which they are enacted may vary. An earthquake may bring down actual buildings and shake the foundations of a city. Or it may be a symbol of a state of upheaval in a country's material foundations, reflected in a severely shaken economy. A volcano may be a concrete eruption of ash and lava, such as the violent cataclysm of Krakatoa. Or it may be an internal collective psychosis, a sudden eruption of long-buried poisons, rage and tribal vendettas such as we have witnessed in what was once called Yugoslavia. The advent of the Antichrist may, as portrayed in medieval religious literature, be the arrival of a particularly evil individual who creates great destruction. Or the Antichrist may be a state of consciousness, as Goethe portrayed in his figure of Mephistopheles – a condition of negativity, resentment, hopelessness, self-deception, and cowardice that leads to a hell on Earth no less bleak than anything imagined in an afterlife.

We know that Nostradamus used both clairvoyant vision and astrology to formulate his prophecies of the future. His *Centuries* have never been out of print since their first publication in the 16th century, for it is a human characteristic to long to know what awaits us so that we can be prepared. Most interpretations of Nostradamus' prophecies do not avail themselves of the astrological knowledge that he possessed, and that would have allowed him to achieve a level of accuracy impossible for clairvoyant vision alone. Most interpreters of Nostradamus also do not avail themselves of the important psychological insight that events may be emotional rather than physical, inner as well as outer, subtle rather than obvious, and – perhaps most importantly – able to be influenced in their level and quality of expression (if not in their essential meaning and timing) according to the level and quality of consciousness brought to bear on them by human awareness, integrity, and choice.

The astrology of the collective – those cycles that reflect movements and change in nations, leaders, and world events – is based upon the same principles as the astrology of the individual. Astrology is not concerned with "fated" events. It is the study of those patterns that reflect the meaning of a particular time. An individual birth horoscope does not predict the literal course of the person's life. It reflects that person's essential character, and therefore the typical ways in which he or she will react to life's challenges. It also reflects the natural timing of the person – the times of growth, consolidation, upheaval and conflict, tranquillity,

Prophecy during the time of Nostradamus was a serious matter, and given authenticity by various sources. One such source was the Oracle at Delphi at the Castalian Spring in Greece where thousands would visit to find wisdom and truth.

and productivity. Not all plants produce their flowers and fruits at the same time. Nor do human beings, who are far more diverse in their natures than any other kingdom of nature. When working intelligently with astrology, one is considering the nature of the individual and the most creative ways in which that person can develop and express what he or she is, so that constructive choices can be made and blind destructiveness of self or others avoided as much as possible. When working intelligently with the birth horoscope of a nation, one is considering precisely the same thing – an entity with an innate character and a set of predisposed responses to life's challenges. Abilities and innate conflicts are reflected in that nation's chart, as are the most likely periods for growth, expansion, conflict, or crisis. An individual has within him or her a cast of psychic characters – an aggressive instinct, a longing for love, a particular quality of leadership or initiative, a special contribution to make on the creative level, and a characteristic defense system that guards against outside intrusion. A nation, too, has a cast of inner characters, played out by its politicians and its people – an aggressive instinct that fights wars, a longing for relationships that lead to alliances with other nations, a style of leadership that colors the choice of government, a special creative contribution to make, and a defense system that dictates how that nation will protect its boundaries from intrusion.

The astrological interpretations in this book are intended to supplement, enhance, and clarify the interpretations of Nostradamus' prophecies. The planetary patterns that reflect our movement into the next century do not describe the end of the world, nor any holocaust that will wipe out civilization. As might be expected, they reflect a heady mixture of new challenges and old conflicts, new crises and old problems, and a profound opportunity for creating a far more enlightened world. Nostradamus would have known about the changing of the astrological ages from Pisces to Aquarius at the end of the 20th century, for the ancient Greeks discovered the phenomenon of the precession of the equinoxes long before. Nostradamus would not have known about the new planets discovered in post-Enlightened times – Uranus, Neptune, and Pluto – but he would have been able to draw on a tradition of millennia

VIRGO

Opposite ~ another important aspect of 16th century "science," with which we have largely lost touch during the 20th century, was the study of alchemy. As part of his varied knowledge, Nostradamus would have been keenly aware of alchemical practices such as those proposed by the 15th century monk-alchemist George Ripley. The detail opposite shows "Ripley's Scroll," a lithographic reproduction illustrating the eight stages of transmutation that were believed to be part of the process of change in matter from base "metal" to enlightened "gold."

explaining the meaning of the other planets and their cycles, thus availing himself of a tool for great insight to clarify his visions. The modern astrologer, however, can add new knowledge to cast light on these visions. What no one – not even Nostradamus himself – can do is predict on what level these great collective patterns will express themselves. Is the Great Prince a real person? Or is he a capacity for enlightened decision-making and self-knowledge that begins to make itself known among individuals as well as nations in the 21st century? Is the oft-mentioned "pestilence" AIDS? Or is it the kind of psychic miasma that afflicts so many modern people trapped in the dreary cycle of a purposeless life?

Perhaps the answer to whether the astrological movements that accompany our transition into the next century manifest themselves as worldly disasters or internal breakthroughs depends ultimately on each one of us. A collective is, after all, a group of individuals. While the birth horoscope of a nation may describe a particular coloration of attitude and style, any individual can bring his or her own power of discernment and choice to collective issues. It is we who choose and "dethrone" our leaders; we who support, admittedly or not, the horror of the concentration camp or the smug morality of the religiously "evolved." And nations, like people, can go through times of suffering and can emerge more mature, more compassionate, and more whole. Like an individual, a nation can undergo a state of breakdown, that if properly understood and "treated" can lead to a far more creative future.

The prophecies of Nostradamus as presented in this volume do not foretell any fixed and unalterable future. Nor do they suggest that we are wandering, blind and impotent, toward the edge of the abyss. Instead, they reflect what has always been true of human beings – that while certain innate patterns may be unavoidable, we can work with such patterns in constructive or destructive ways according to how well we understand ourselves. In the final analysis, it is, after all, up to us what kind of future we create as we move with such bewilderment into the next millennium.

Dr. Liz Greene, Oxford, England
September 1992.

Introduction

DR. NOSTRADAME & THE PATH TO ENLIGHTENMENT

Above ~ Nostradamus

Opposite *~ without the powerful influence of Catherine de Medici, Queen to Henry II of France, Nostradamus would probably never have reached the fame and fortune he did during his life. Although still adhering to a public image of Catholic faith, Catherine practiced the "dark" rituals of black magic, prophecy and clairvoyance within her private chambers in Paris. Her interest in Nostradamus arose out of his successful predictions concerning her family, and in particular the death of King Henry, which the prophet predicted three years before the event.*

H E WAS A LITTLE UNDER MEDIUM HEIGHT, of robust body, nimble and vigorous. He had a large and open forehead, a straight and even nose, gray eyes that were generally pleasant but that blazed when he was angry, and a visage both severe and smiling, such that along with his severity a great humanity could be seen; his cheeks were ruddy, even in his old age, his beard was long and thick, his health good and hearty (except in his old age), and all his senses acute and complete. His mind was good and lively, understanding easily what he wanted; his judgment was subtle, his memory quite remarkable. By nature he was taciturn, thinking much and saying little, though speaking very well in the proper time and place: for the rest, vigilant, prompt, and impetuous, prone to anger, patient in labor. He slept only four to five hours. He praised and loved freedom of speech and showed himself joyous and facetious, as well as biting, in his joking. He approved of the ceremonies of the Roman Church and held to the Catholic faith and religion, outside of which, he was convinced, there was no salvation; he reproved grievously those who, withdrawn from its bosom, abandoned themselves to eating and drinking of the sweetness and liberties of the foreign and damned doctrines, affirming that they would come to bad and pernicious end. I do not want to forget to say that he engaged willingly in fasts, prayers, alms, and patience; he abhorred vice and chastised it severely; I can remember his giving to the poor, toward whom he was very liberal and charitable, often making use of these words, drawn from the Holy Scriptures, "Make friends of the riches of iniquity."

Jean-Aime de Chavigny

In the early 16th century there were no nationally distributed newspapers. It wasn't possible to turn on a television and watch people dying

Above ~ *Part of his personal understanding of the importance of human life was exemplified in Nostradamus'work as a doctor and curer of the dreaded bubonic plague, which raged across Europe during the 16th century.*

Opposite ~ *Hermes Trismegistus – the first known record of the concept of synergy – that the universe corresponds with everything on Earth – was already understood in the 2nd century CE. The Greek "Emerald Tablet" of Trismegistus was inscribed with the words: "What is above is like what is below and what is below is like what is above, so that the miracle of the One may be accomplished."*

of the bubonic plague. Information traveled as fast as the fastest horse – about a hundred miles a day at best. And if there was water to cross then the story could take months or even years to arrive on your doorstep. And yet, the prophet and doctor, Michel de Nostradame (known mostly now by the Latin version of his name – Nostradamus) was known throughout the European world as one of the most extraordinary individuals of that time – a time of radical change in religion and politics: the beginning of the Reformation, as it is known, when Luther nailed his 95 theses to the castle church of Wittenburg in 1517; a time when the medieval world of Europe was turning into the Renaissance world of art and expression; a time when freedom was beginning to mean something. Catholicism, however, was still an enormously powerful force in the West. It carried not only the mysticism that gave it power from God through the Pope, but also a great political and military force directed by the same "King" of the Church. An individual needed only to speak of something regarded by the Church as heresy, and he might soon find himself under interrogation or risk punishment by the Spanish Inquisition. In this sense almost all of the countries of Europe were like the worst dictatorships of the 20th century – all in the name of God. For this was the Piscean Age – the age of miracles, of blind belief, an age that had dominated the planet Earth for 1,500 years, and was then slowly moving out of Pisces into the cusp with Aquarius, as we shall see.

One of the most extraordinary characters of this age lived in the small town of Salon in Provence, now Southern France. The prophet Nostradamus was clairvoyant, an astrologer, a doctor of medicine, a cosmetician, a confectioner, and, as we will learn from his verses, a considerable historian. He was, by birth, also a Jew and by the training of his grandfather, an alchemist. And later in life as a prominent figure of the early 16th century, Nostradamus put himself constantly at risk.

As a clairvoyant, because of his reputation as a clairvoyant, he was sought by the Spanish Inquisition and the French royal family. He was also at risk from those who might be involved in his prophecies, specific

ΘΕΟC

people who were named so precisely in those extraordinary verses within *Centuries*. As an astrologer he trod somewhat confused ground, for at that time astrology and astronomy had not yet been separated, and astrology was both occult and science, so was regarded as potentially heretical by the Church – only God saw the heavens. As a doctor of medicine he risked his life everyday while walking among sufferers of the dreaded bubonic plague, administering dried rose-petal lozenges to his patients – then the most outrageous of cures, totally against established medical practice.

As a prophet and cosmetician he became involved with one of the most scandalous royal families in Europe – that of Catherine de Medici, being summoned to Paris to predict the precarious future of a powerful political group, and at the same time to administer his cosmetic cures for their troubled bodies. Only his concoctions of jam and marmalade, for which he also became famous, were truly safe activities for this extraordinary polymath.

Nostradamus' grandfather, a successful corn merchant, renounced the family's Judaic faith in favor of the safer Catholicism when the boy was only nine years old. His grandfather taught him Greek, Latin, Hebrew, and astronomy/astrology based on the Copernican theories that the world was round and circled the Sun. These ideas would get Galileo into trouble some years later because the Church maintained that the world was flat. The fundamental basis of astrology was founded on the Greek understanding that the heavens corresponded with everything and everyone on Earth. That, in effect, everything was interconnected. The earliest known origin of this concept is the Emerald Tablet of Hermes Trismegistus from the 2nd century CE that bears the inscription, "What is above is like what is below and what is below is like what is above, so

that the miracle of the One may be accomplished." This is highly sophisticated thinking that only today is being scientifically proven through the new discoveries of quantum physics. All astrology is based on this understanding, the intuitive perception that the cosmos is one interconnected lifeform with various parts that reflect each other at any one given moment. That when an individual is born, therefore, there is a cogent picture of that life, the personality, and the place in the heavens. The occult beliefs that went with this, and with which Michel was certainly familiar, were in turn based on a concept of cyclic events, that all things returned to their beginning and moved in an everlasting continuum. If the world was flat then occultism was worthless – a belief that the Catholic Church wished to maintain, but one that almost all intelligent individuals of the time quietly denied, even up to the highest levels of society. The Church therefore also found astrology threatening because any insight into such correspondences would give individuals insight into the cycles of life, thereby negating the need for the priests.

Science in Nostradamus' life was therefore mixed with magic, and it was magic derived from the most ancient and pagan practices – practices that were kept alive even within the French court of Catherine de Medici.

It is important to remember, however, that Nostradamus was primarily a scientist. He regarded astrology/astronomy as the "Celestial Science" and required a precise scientific analysis for all the ideas that were of interest to him. He states quite clearly in his "Preface by M. Nostradamus to his Prophecies," written for his son Csar, that "...leave you this reminder, after my death, for the benefit of all men, of what the divine spirit has vouchsafed me to know by means of astronomy."

There is little doubt that he possessed extraordinary clairvoyant gifts, but in all his writings he consistently attributes these to God, as though he worked simply as a channel for a higher entity. In his training to be a physician in Montpellier, this analytical tendency would have been emphasized, and, from 1525, when he obtained his bachelor's degree in

ARIES

Opposite ~ *of all the influences that Nostradamus used to become one of the most unique characters in our history, astrology was the most important. The use of "Celestial Science" to overlay the complexity of clairvoyant prophecy, brought his view of the future into sharper perspective and there is no doubt he was a master of it.*
The picture opposite is taken from the title page of "Dialogo di Galileo Galilei," published in 1632 by the Medici family, who supported Galileo's work in Florence. The book led to Galileo's trial which arose out of his suggestion that the world was not the center of the universe.

medicine, he practiced his newfound skills as an itinerant healer in the towns and cities around Toulouse, Bordeaux, and Avignon where he found enormous success in curing the plague.

So the life of this man was beset by powerful contradictions. And it may have been just these contradictions that brought his more famous gifts to the forefront of his later life.

While practicing as a doctor he quickly made friendships in high places, in particular with a religious philosopher of the time named Julius Caesar Scalinger. He settled down in Agen at Scalinger's request and married a lady from local society (we are not given her name), with whom he had two children. Everything seemed to be settled and perhaps his life might have been normal, a successful doctor working in his local area. But this was not to be.

All in the space of only one year, everything in Nostradamus' life burst apart. While he worked relentlessly and successfully to cure hundreds of people of the plague, his wife and children died of this same ghastly disease, right before his eyes. His inability to cure his own family discredited him in the eyes of the local dignitaries, including Scalinger. His wife's parents sued him for the dowry they had given at the marriage, and the local "branch" of the Spanish Inquisition began paying closer attention to the activities of this famous doctor.

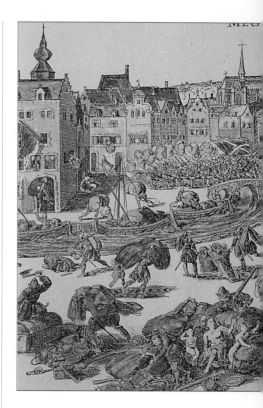

It was as if he entered a period of "ashes," a dark night of the soul, in which he began a major transformation. He was forced to leave Agen and he took to wandering the roads of France and Italy for six years before he settled down again to produce the beginnings of what today we know as *The Centuries* – the twelve volumes of his prophecies covering thousands of years into the future.

Nostradamus' prophecies are the most extraordinary in the entire history of mankind, with the possible exception of the prophecies of the Bible itself. No other prophet covers such a massive span of history.

The work that he fulfilled during the period after his wanderings, following what was almost certainly a major transformation, resulted in the prophecies that have been kept alive in continuous publications over the

*Medieval Europe during the time of
Nostradamus' life was a place of
considerable suffering. When the plague
wasn't ravaging the towns and outlying
areas, the Spanish Inquisition was burning
witches and torturing heretics. It is not
surprising therefore that the writings of
Nostradamus are filled with forebodings of
fear and dread.*

past 400 years. Their ability to tell us something about our future is as much an enigma at the end of this millennium as it ever was.

The Centuries contain 965 verses (quatrains) written in the latter part of his life. They were eventually composed and published in ten volumes, some during his life and some after. It is from this extraordinary series of enigmatic verses, and from his other writings, that many interpreters over the last four centuries have drawn their inspiration, and from which we also will attempt to see the future. Each interpreter has selected various of the verses and some have commented on all of them, where possible applying them to the different times since Nostradamus' lifetime. Where verses cannot be applied to events in our past, they are taken to be about our future and it is within this enigmatic realm that we will apply ourselves in the pages of this book. It is not possible to include all the verses that appear to be concerned with the next few decades, simply because of available space within this book, given that there is also an extensive illustrated aspect. The author has therefore selected "quatrains" (verses) that can be interpreted according to various subjects which are most relevant to us, such as politics, religion, natural phenomena and matters of social interest. The verses are further divided to apply to different countries of the world, and in each case, with the help of the astrologer Dr. Liz Greene, the natal charts of these countries are provided to add greater accuracy so that we may acquire a clearer vision of how the near future will unfold. Each time a quatrain is quoted in the original French version, a number appears – for example C1 1. This signifies the place within *The Centuries* that the particular quatrain can be found – Century (volume) 1, verse 1.

We know that Nostradamus could not have concocted his predictions purely through clairvoyance or astrology alone, though his clairvoyant gifts were perhaps the spiritual source of his power to "see." In order to bring these strange ideas down to earth and make them a little more rational, he used the "Celestial Science." We know that Nostradamus was deeply ensconced in the processes of astrology because many of his verses make direct references to astrological changes, and, in addition,

Opposite ~ *"Map of the Sun's Path" – from Andreas Cellarius's "Atlas Coelestis seu Harmonia Macrocosmica" published in 1660.*

Nostradamus would have had access to similar charts as part of his research work into the astrological movements of the heavenly bodies, though he was working within astronomy/astrology almost a century before Galileo brought his telescope into use for the benefit of star-gazers. The prophet/astrologer was, however, living at the same time as the still more famous Nicolaus Copernicus, whose "Six Books on the Revolutions of the Celestial Orbs" was published in 1543. Using such maps of the heavens, Nostradamus was able to move forward in time to follow the synergy between the planets in the Solar system and the people of Earth.

from the records that were kept of his library by his secretary, de Chauvegny, we know that he studied Greek astrology. There is some hint in his writings that he disliked amateur astrologers, but this does not indicate that he disputed the powers of the planets to see the future. But what we need to remember, and what we will find within the coming pages, is that this man, for all his brilliance and diversity, eventually became a real master, a kind of enlightened magician. The evidence gathered shows someone who was very down to earth, very simple, and very wise. Interpreters have put many different characteristics onto the man, some of them unnecessarily complex for, when we look behind the poetic verses of his predictions, we actually find something much simpler than many would imagine. In fact, it is the purpose of this book to show that the quatrains are mostly entirely straightforward.

Nostradamus couched all his predictions in metaphors and riddles, but the modern interpreters have often attributed a greater degree of complexity to them than is actually present. Many of the pieces of the puzzle are based very simply in historical references that were familiar to Nostradamus, as we shall see. And the key factor is the familiarity to him, for the historical references are not necessarily at all familiar to us. Many of the words that have puzzled interpreters and commentators are simply names of individuals who were contemporary to Nostradamus or well-known from his past. We offer, therefore, in the pages of this book, some quite startling new material that brings the enigmatic verses considerably closer to our comprehension than they have been before now.

As part of the interpretations and as a general basis for the view of the near future that the prophet gave us, we will use the astrological readings and charts that Nostradamus would have had access to. Astrology has become more sophisticated in the 20th century, largely because of the discovery of new planets since Nostradamus' lifetime. We will use this additional skill also, but for the most part what we can show is what Nostradamus knew, and what he would have implemented into his plan for the future of mankind as he saw it centuries before it occurred.

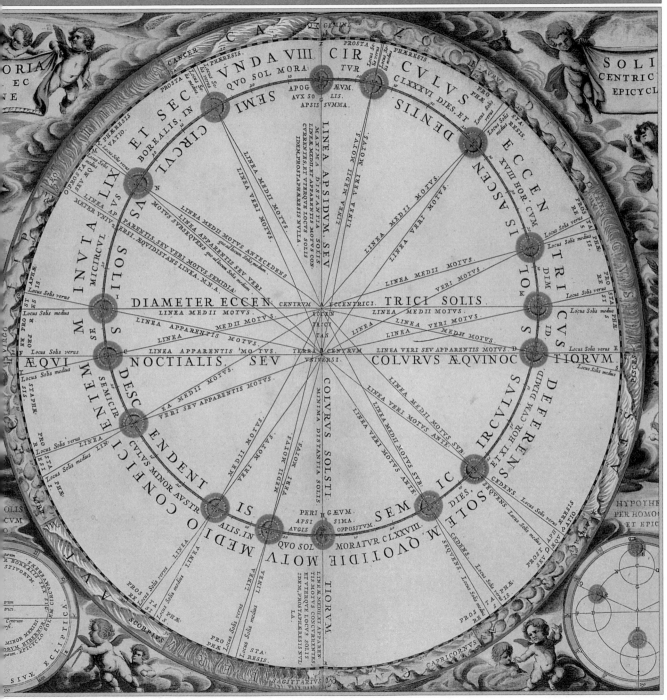

21

The Pragmatic Diviner

THROUGHOUT THE COMING PAGES, it will quickly become evident that interpreting Nostradamus' quatrains is like a detective hunt. Clues are scattered throughout the short verses like those left behind by a thief in the night. All manner of historical elements are added to the words, so that in effect the interpreter must get under the skin of the prophet and try to think as he might have done, trying to place him or herself within the time contemporary to Nostradamus.

It must be added, however, that the task of making good sense out of Nostradamus can seem sometimes frustrating and long-winded at the outset. It takes time to become familiar with his methods, and looking back at previous attempts seems only to confuse the situation further, as each interpreter appears to have a different idea about how the verses should be translated and then understood. Take the following for example:

Estant assis de nuict secret estude,
Seul, reposé sur la selle d'aerain?
Flambe exique sortant de solitude,
Fait prospérer qui n'est à croire vain.
C1 1

La verge en mains mise au milieu de Branches,
De l'onde il moulle et le limbe et le pied,
Un peur et voix fremissent par les manches,
Spledeur divine le divin près s'assied.
C1 2

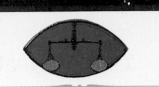

The scene in this picture is about as close as we could expect to get to a medieval apothecary's laboratory. The reconstruction, similar to one that can be found in the Swiss Museum of Pharmaceutical History in Basel, contains all the tools that an alchemist would have needed for his experiments.

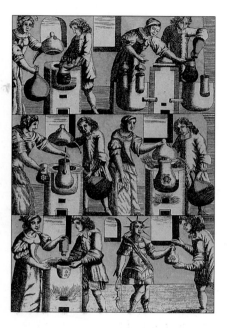

Above ~ *an illustration from the "Mutus Liber" – The Wordless Book, an alchemical study published in 1677 and thought to have been designed by Jacob Saulet. The picture is entitled, "The Making of the Flower of Fixity from the elements."*
Nostradamus' verses, in many senses, are alchemical in nature, for they transform over long periods of time, from the base metal in which they began life during the 16th century, to greater and greater gold as we come to understand them better.

"Sitting alone at night in secret study at rest on a stool (or tripod) of brass a slight flame leaves the solitude and prospers that which should not be accepted emptily."

"The wand (or caduceus) in hand, placed between the branches he shapes the edge and foot in fear he trembles as the feeble-minded. Splendour divine the divine sits near."

Interpreters down the ages have bounced around these extraordinary, enigmatic verses in almost every direction. They carry great importance because they are the first quatrains that Nostradamus wrote in *The Centuries*. In addition they tell us about the way he conducted his prophetic sessions using occult or clairvoyant techniques. For 20th century people, such activities are somewhat intimidating because our age is not one that contains much natural magic. Instinctual understanding is treated with suspicion because of our insistence on scientific or rational explanations for everything. At the same time we yearn for more magic, and therefore give some eras of past history a high degree of importance for their magical content. To Nostradamus, magic and the occult would have been a fairly normal aspect of life.

As far as this verse is concerned, all interpreters have looked under a very strong magnifying glass, perhaps unnecessarily.

First of all, the original version was written in two different languages, Latin and old French. Some of the words could therefore mean at least two different things, such as the word "manches" that is here translated as "feeble-minded" from the old French word. Some translators have taken it to mean "sleeve" from the modern French word "manche" and then have gone on to make the sense of this line quite differently from the way it is translated on this page.

Second, various classical references appear in the text. For example

Apparatus used by
17th century alchemists.
Above ~ A "Kerotakis", a
Greek alchemical device for
exposing metals to chemical vapors.
Below ~ A Caduceus, magic wand of
Mercury, often kept by doctors in
the Middle Ages.

the word "verge" is a Latin word that we here translate as "wand." Nostradamus would have carried a doctor's "caduceus" with him, a device that derived from the magic wand of Mercury, traditionally kept by doctors in the Middle Ages as a symbol of their profession – so that this "verge" could have been his caduceus in use as a kind of solemn device in the same way we might now use a precious item for good fortune. This has been generously translated in some cases straight to "divining rod," implying sorcery or some sepulchral power source.

But if we look a little more closely there really isn't any implication of sorcery in this verse. The word "secret" in the first line causes the 20th Century adrenalin to flow. What is this secret? This is then allied in the mind to the implications of sorcery. We read so much in the press about secret black magic practices that we assume Nostradamus' secret to be related to some very shady behavior not far from the boiling cauldron of the witch's den. The first line has often been translated to mean, "Seated alone at night in my secret study". In other words the study (a private room used for work) is secret. A less dramatic version would be, "Sitting alone at night in secret study", meaning that he is alone and working on something secret. Simple enough, and nothing much to do with the occult. The second line is often translated to mean, "Alone, he rested over a brass tripod." Brass tripods in the time of Nostradamus were often used to support brass bowls full of water, that in turn were used to "see" the future by "reading" the water. This evokes a scene perhaps similar to many we have watched in movies about sorcerers and magicians, in which there is a wizard with a pointed hat and long robe who gazes in a fascinated trance into a misty picture on the surface of the water.

The moment we turn the tripod into a stool it is less dramatic but perhaps more realistic. Here was Nostradamus, probably dressed in comfortable robes, sitting on a brass stool. What could be simpler? He was at his studies, not casting horrendous black magic spells.

But now the verse begins to take some shape, as in the third line we

Alchemy was part of the cosmic order. Alchemical symbols are seen in this illustration against a fabulous background of universal synergy, from Mylius's "Opus Medico-chymicum" published in 1618. There is much debate and fascination surrounding the ways in which Nostradamus worked his amazing prophecies – whether they were the result of drugs, hypnosis, black magic or clairvoyance. The likely truth is that it was a mixture of all these things, for the cosmic order was seen to contain all magic, together with the past, present and future.

read about the candle that, "leaves the solitude and prospers that which should not be accepted emptily." In this line, Nostradamus writes like the poet he is. He also indicates that there is perhaps more to what he is saying than the simple words on the page.

He is studying something secret, but what is the secret? He is studying by the light of a "slight flame" – why "slight"? The French word "exigue" is similar to another word in Latin that implies that we are looking at symbolic meanings. In fact we can, if we look closely at almost all of Nostradamus' quatrains, understand that rather than being a magician with some weird and wonderful power of prophecy, he is a brilliant clairvoyant and scientific astrologer with a powerful sense of the symbolic.

We can take this even a step further and say that the famous quatrains that have generally been interpreted to predict only specific events of war and disaster, actually have much broader references across a far wider spectrum of subjects. Perhaps we might begin to see this astonishing man in a rather less gloomy light as we learn more about him and widen our attitudes from those provided by interpreters who were perhaps conditioned by the presence of war in their own times.

And, finally, one last point that may help us with the process of seeing into the future. A great confusion that confronts the interpreter of the quatrains in *The Centuries* is that they appear to be totally at random throughout. There is no sense of order. They are not, for example, arranged in a chronological time sequence. This would have been extremely convenient. If we could simply have ticked off the verses as they came true, we could know what was to come next. Unfortunately

this tends not to be the way of the irrational process of prediction. We do not yet understand most of the things that happen in the present, let alone things that are being predicted way into the future.

• But if we look closely we do begin to find a kind of rationality in the way the verses are grouped together. For Nostradamus appears to set his verses together according to topics in some cases. There are certain more common areas of interest, such as religion. We find many quatrains on this subject, with a particular similarity to the predictions of the Book of Revelations in the use of language and symbols, i.e. blood, plagues, famine, altars, earthquakes, and the like. But, in addition, carefully tucked away, very often at the beginning of each *Century*, we find other subjects, such as women, family, relationships, and even a treasure hunt. These more intimate verses bring us down to earth and paint a picture, as we will see in later chapters, that is both fascinating, revealing, and extremely tender-hearted.

Above left ~ *St. John the Evangelist in the Apocalypse with the Dragon in the Abyss, the 13th century version of man's fight to survive.*
Opposite top ~ *a depiction from the 16th century of Nostradamus with Catherine de Medici performing pagan rites of divination, absolutely against the laws of the Catholic Inquisition. Much of what Nostradamus wrote appears to be filled with doom and disaster, from dreaded plagues through to end-of-world scenarios. His interests seem always to lie with cataclysm and the fall of mankind. Perhaps this is why he is so popular during the last years of this century, because we feel sure of our own downfall - we are somehow a mirror of the old medieval times in which the prophet lived.*

The Astrological Backdrop

GEMINI

TAURUS

A S MENTIONED, the use of Nostradamus' quatrains as a form of prediction will be backed up in this book with the use of modern astrology. As students of prophecy we are sadly inadequate in the 20th century. The various disciplines of reasoning and our reliance on the mind as a "sensible" (as opposed to sensitive) tool have combined to make us virtually ignorant of the instinctive processes of magic and miracles. The arts of the alchemist and the wizard have been largely lost. But one area of ancient knowledge that has survived is astrology – suitably translated into the modern age with a set of scientific rules. This we do understand, so that the presence of an astrological background, provided in this case by world famous astrologer, Dr. Liz Greene, will help us to set the scene of our prophecies, and at least give a stronger sense of authenticity to the complex tapestry that Dr. de Nostradame set in motion on our behalf in the 16th Century.

We will draw up astrological charts for the United States of America, using the precise birth date of the country. We will do the same for other places such as the United Kingdom, and the former Soviet Union, Germany, and other parts of Europe. We will draw up charts for major personalities involved in our religious future, and for situations that will unfold during the next years. This way we will be able to use both Nostradamus' quatrains, and the astrological readings that he would also have charted, as a powerful combination to help us look into our own future.

The subjects to be covered all have their sources in today's headlines; in politics, religion, social unrest, natural disaster, the body, mind, and spirit, but also concerning the exploration of less grand aspects of society in the future. Most of Nostradamus' interpreters have kept away from matters such as family, marriage, psychology, social order, and relationships. Perhaps because the verses appear to be about major themes, they have almost always been seen to be in relation to wars, famines, and national affairs rather than more "homely" matters. But, as we have

In fact our period of history is not so dissimilar to that of the pre-Renaissance era. We still find the homeless living in doorways in freezing cold temperatures without work, money or security. We still suffer from dreadful plagues and awesome wars.

explored already, when we look more closely we find that the words can often refer to these things in some detail by use of symbols, and also by examining them on the level of the "inner" rather than the "outer" life, and it will be this detail that we will see unfold in the coming pages.

We will look at what Nostradamus would have seen as the Aquarian Age, as it influences our lives today, and how it will continue to force us to live in a world that is constantly in flux for at least the next fifty years. We take a more precise look at the transit of Pluto through the signs of Scorpio and Sagittarius, that have the property of bringing the poisons and corruptions of life to the surface before a healing and transformative process can begin. Like a kind of cleansing cure, this transit will work in the world to prepare the way for something new. We can see this evidenced in the collapse of Communism, the problems in organized religion, and the various wars around the world. Nostradamus had access to the astrological information concerning the Age of Aquarius, so that much of what he wrote would have been gleaned from this knowledge. But more of that later.

We will be looking at specific events in the future such as the transformation of the organized religions into something completely new, the major changes that we can expect in the United States, and the increasing dominance of Europe as it becomes a world force. And what we will see is a new pattern emerging as the Aquarian Age takes its path from the cusp into the main body of the Age itself, that most astrologers maintain is happening during these last years of the 20th Century.

The procession of the equinoxes is not sharp, with beginnings and ends. They merge into one another gradually, so that we retain characteristics of the old Piscean Age as well as the new ones from the Aquarian. The cusp of the Piscean and Aquarian Ages began their changeover around the beginning of the 20th Century, the age when science and reason took a stronger foothold over our lives, shedding blind belief and unquestioned faith. As we move forward more and more into the Aquarian Age itself, we find that these are the years that Nostradamus foretold to be a thousand years of peace, and in this book we will see why, for this age of turmoil we are present does not last forever.

But it's not over yet. There is still a great deal of turmoil to come, a great deal of change and unrest on this rapidly developing planet. But according to Nostradamus and the astrological indications for the future, the end of this millennium and the early years of the next will see some very exciting new ideas born out of the chaos of the present.

Chapter 1

THE MASTER'S VISION

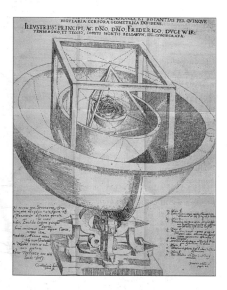

Le divin verbe donrra a la substance,
Comprins ciel, terre, or occult ai faict mystique:
Corps, ame esprit ayant toute puissance,
Tant soubs ses pieds comme au siege Celique.

C3 2

*"The divine verb will give to the substance that which contains the
sky and the land (heaven and earth), occult gold to the mystic deed.
Body, soul and mind are all powerful. All is beneath his feet, like
the seat of the heavens."*

IN THIS FIRST CHAPTER we take a broad look at the prevailing astrological combinations of which Nostradamus would have been aware as affecting our near future, and see how they fit with some relevant quatrains. On the broadest astrological scale we will first examine the "astrological ages" upon which all the prophet's works were based.

Nostradamus' view of the future, being set against the correspondences of alchemical transformation, clairvoyant divination, occult magic and religion, came straight out of the cosmic order that was his greatest interest, and that of all intelligent thinkers of the time. It was not simply a matter of the day-to-day positions of the planets and suns, but also a much wider scale of movement occuring over thousands of years into the future.

These grand cycles of life were bigger than anything mankind had sampled, indeed one cycle could cover almost half of the civilized world's development, like a massive stride across time.

*The picture is of a model of the solar system
as interlinking solids which was proposed by
Johannes Kepler as part of an astrological
proposal printed in 1597.*

Opposite *~ a design illustrated to show the
stages of the perfection of the alchemical
stone and its cosmic correspondences. It is
taken from the "Cabala" by Stefan
Michelspacher, 1616.*

*All this sets the scene for the beginning of
our hunt for answers to Nostradamus'
fascinating verses.*

IGNIS.

AERIS.

AQVÆ.

TERRÆ.

VWIWV

TINCTVR.
COAGVLATION.
DISTILLATION.
PVTREFACTION.
SOLVTION.
SVBLIMATION.
CALTINATION.

The Astrological Ages

Opposite ~ *an illustration of the predicted great flood of 1574 which was believed would occur during an astrological "line-up" when all the twelve planets would be located in Pisces, the sign of the fishes. The print is taken from the Johannes Stoeffler Almanac published in 1504.*
Needless to say, the flood did not occur as prophecy seems not only to rely upon astrology for its success.
We lie, during the last years of the 20th century, within a tiny first step of the Aquarian Age, an Age that will continue for 2000 years into our future. Nostradamus was able to "see" the whole of this Age and made predictions stretching right across it.

FOR NOSTRADAMUS, and still for modern astrologers today, time is divided into "astrological ages" and these different ages correspond to the different signs of the Zodiac running backwards through them. Each astrological age lasts for approximately 2000 years, with some variations according to the size of the constellation. The complete cycle of all the different ages, known as the "Great Year," covers a period of 25,000 years. For example, the Aries/Pisces cusp (i.e. that period of change between the constellation of Aries and that of Pisces) commenced in approximately 50 BCE and lasted until approximately 50 CE.

The Piscean Age began in approximately 0 CE and lasts until approximately 2000 CE. The Pisces/Aquarius cusp, overlapping with the Pisces and Aquarius ages, occurs between approximately 1950 and 2050, with the Aquarian Age "proper" continuing from around 2000 to 4000. Following the Aquarian Age we will then pass into the Aquarius/ Capricorn cusp which will continue from approximately 3550 to 4050. This entire, vast period of human life on Earth was "visible" to Nostradamus, who would also have been aware of its astrological implications.

In this chapter, therefore, we will take a look at the implications of the Aquarian Age, according to Nostradamus' predictions, and also use the astrological data that he possessed, which 20th century astrologers have improved upon with a greater knowledge of the existence of "new" planets such as Uranus and Pluto, which Nostradamus did not know of. Even Galileo's telescope could not see so far into the skies, one hundred years later.

Nevertheless we can assume that Nostradamus was completely aware of the broader patterns of the move from Pisces to Aquarius through the grand plan of the "Great Years."

Following this, in the rest of the chapters in the book, we will turn to the more detailed task of examining the different quatrains and their application to specific events in our future.

The Marriage of Pisces & Aquarius

NOSTRADAMUS, THE ASTROLOGER, would have been aware of the broad astrological influences of the sign of Aquarius in our age. To him and his age, the leading planet that would dominate the Aquarian Age was that of Saturn. This would have indicated to him that the turn of the end of the 20th Century was to be a time of penetrating, scientific, and philosophical reason that would prompt questions rather than acceptance. Saturn also implies the need for control and the structuring of natural resources and an intelligent use of world resources to make the present more bearable (in contrast to Jupiter, that ruled the Piscean Age, that suggested faith in God's bounty and an overdeveloped belief in the afterlife).

In mythology, Saturn was the god of agriculture and presided over the golden age and the laws of good farming and conservation of the earth.

Above ~ Saturn on his chariot with dragons. A 16th century rendering of the mythology surrounding the marriage of astrology and astronomy.

Opposite top ~ a 16th century engraving of the green lion eating the Sun. Such an illustration demonstrates the extraordinary complexity of alchemical thinking. The green lion was a symbol for aqua regia (royal water) – a mixture of nitric and hydrochloric acids that would dissolve gold, symbolized by the Sun. The gold would often contain copper which, when dissolved would color the acid green, thus the green lion. Such was the vivid nature of the depiction of a simple chemical reaction during this time of magic and discovery.

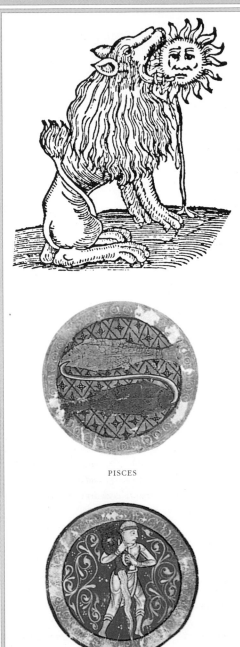

PISCES

AQUARIUS

The Piscean Age, which very much influenced Nostradamus' lifetime, was one of blind belief, of unquestioning religious faith, of a belief in miracles and magic as the very foundation of life. This gave birth to both religious dogma, to the idea that God was "out there" and not to be questioned – a structure that dominated the whole of the Middle Ages and a large part of the Renaissance period – but also to the actual existence of miracles and magic; of Jesus walking on the water, of alchemical magic, and of the dominance of unreasoned and often fantastic events.

The Aquarian Age, by contrast, will eventually bring us out of this miraculous, unreasoned basis for life into a time when nothing goes unquestioned, and science delves into all matters and asks the most piercing questions. Philosophy and reason pluck the petals from every rose and dissect every cell of existence. Each process of discovery is a process of movement – a verb rather than a noun.

The domination of Saturn also gives rise to certain flavor of political revolution, for in the area of social leadership there is also the constant process of questioning. We have seen already this century that there has hardly been a single decade when political revolution was not in the headlines: The Spanish Civil War, the two World Wars, Vietnam, Communism, Yugoslavia, The European Community. This revolutionary process is different in this century from revolutions of the past, inasmuch as they have little to do with any idealistic concepts, such as was the case with the French Revolution. This century's political changes seem more to do with despotic rulership, such as in Russia, the USSR, and Germany, thus reflecting the negative side of the mythic Saturn who ate his own children in order to prevent them from succeeding him according to the natural cycles of time.

Another important characteristic of the Aquarian definition of life on Earth is that of the collective. There is, and will continue to be, a growth pattern through collective activity rather than individual. Countries move together into continents, or states into nations, as in the case of the United States. The growth of the European countries into the European

Community is a perfect example of the Aquarian tendency towards group activity. The whole ecological movement presently filling the media is another example of the same tendency, and the Gaia movement – the whole Earth movement, the concept of a global community – is the final result of the characteristics of an Aquarian Age.

Nostradamus would have been aware of these characteristics and their application to our times.

These same global concepts also connect us in more intimate ways. We are becoming aware that everything we do, in each part of our lives, connects with every other part. On the most obvious level we can see that if an industrial factory allows waste to flow into rivers, the waters become poisoned. If we spray certain gases into the air, then the ozone layer is damaged. These matters are of the greatest concern to us today.

On a more subtle and personal level, we can apply the same connecting feature of Aquarius to our own lives. If we allow our day-to-day existence to be turgid, unhappy, dishonest, and bored, then the result will be depression and a poor lifestyle. If we believe positively in what we are doing, attempt to do only those things that make us happy, then the result is joy and happiness. In other words, everything we put into existence, we get back in similar form. And it is not simply that such astrological characteristics produce new ways of thinking, but that the whole of human consciousness actually alters. And as consciousness alters, so events transform. During the Piscean Age of miracles, miracles occurred. During the Aquarian Age of change and the penetration of reason, everything is subject to science and reason.

But, we may ask, if everything is scientific and reasonable, why is there so much chaos around right now? The answer is, first, that Aquarius is not only the sign of reason and science but also the sign in which humanity is attempting to master the instinctual world of nature. There are bound to be many scientific breakthroughs that result in radical changes in knowledge and lifestyle. Second, we are now in the cusp of the two signs, coming towards Aquarius. Everything is in flux because we are altering our perception toward an age of change, but it is also in flux because such massive changes create anxiety.

As the human consciousness manifests the characteristics of the Aquarian Age, it also has to deal with the anxieties that such transformation evokes. We are on a cusp of change. The definitions of reality have slipped – church, state, family – and yet the new definitions have not established themselves. Everything seems to be a mess because we are trying to readjust to the new "rules" – rules that demand our blind faith of the past to be in question constantly. And these questions will inevitably lead to answers that will eventually bring some peace of mind. But for the moment that peace of mind is still only a dim light at the end of the tunnel.

And the more powerful the changes, the more likely we are to try to withdraw from them. The unification of the European Community is a perfect example of this. As the tendency grows toward joining together into larger nations and groups of nations, so the tribal instinct comes to the surface to maintain the small groups. We fight to hold onto our national heritages, languages, traditions, even currencies, as these disappear into larger concepts and structures. We are perhaps afraid that the huge collective will stifle the expression and needs of the individual. There have been many empires that have ended up crushing the people that made them, only to collapse into disaster. There are no easy answers to the future. We are groping in the dark for new solutions – the perfect scenarios of the Aquarian Age.

These Aquarian characteristics and their interaction on the cusp between Pisces and Aquarius would also have been evident to Nostradamus. Knowledge of them would, in fact, have led him to write the verse at the top of this chapter. A verse that describes the latter part of this millennium perfectly, and which we will now examine in some detail.

While the strength of the dollar managed to stabilize the world economy up until the 1970's, our present monetary climate is radically changing and the huge and largely invisible empire which the United States has supported with its loans, gifts and what some might accuse, its bribes, is now crumbling and leaving a new power vacuum.

Opposite *~The pomp and sanctified rituals of the old religions no longer disguises some very secular corruption which is gradually eroding the message of the church.*

Religion ~ From Outer to Inner

Nostradamus saw clearly how the Aquarian Age would affect our vision of godliness. We can see this if we look again at the verse that begins this chapter.

"The divine verb will give to the substance that which contains the sky and the land (heaven and Earth), occult gold to the mystic deed. Body, soul and mind are all powerful. All is beneath his feet, like the seat of the heavens."

URING THE LAST FEW YEARS WE HAVE WATCHED the power of the heads of the organized religions diminish. We have watched the Catholic Church being reduced from its original magic and unearthly sanctity to a very earthy and rather unlikely organization with many very human inadequacies. We have seen the holy become human; the almighty priest become fallen and often bedevilled by secret sexual longings and financial failings. Once again we begin to watch as the Piscean era of unquestioned magic turns into the Aquarian era of probing and reasoning. The priest within the Piscean Age, ruled by Jupiter, was the "priest/prophet," the voice of God, and his visionary wisdom and faith provided the moral and religious law that simple mortals were expected to follow. The new priest, within the Aquarian Age, ruled by Saturn, is the "priest/teacher" who is like a rabbi with great knowledge of life born out of his own experience, thus giving him or her an ability to provide practical help to those who would live in the here and now.

The old established Churches can no longer stand up to the piercing gaze of Aquarian analysis as long as the old rules are still applied.

One of the most potent images of the past, in terms of religion, has been that of God in the heavens surrounded by angels and chariots, cherubs hovering above his head, bolts of lightning flashing – mighty forces far greater than ever mankind could muster. Mankind, the puny and powerless creature, unworthy of the virtues of godliness, must wait until heaven's gate to be given everlasting peace and good will. The power of God was always to keep man down until after death. So life was just suffering – "life is hell and then you die." The negative side of Pisces that dominated our past was this passive acceptance and resignation to the misery of the mortal lot, and an excessive focusing on life-after-death as compensation.

None of this stands up to any kind of penetrating gaze. Even on the most mundane level, for an angel to fly more than half an inch off the ground, it would need a sternum four feet out from the front of its chest. Aerodynamics are too advanced to make do with angelic lore. Something new is needed.

There are too many unanswerable questions.

The near future, according to astrological readings and Nostradamus, before the first years of the new millennium are out, is the advent of the "priest/guide," a new kind of religious person, who will act essentially as a simple advisor, even at the highest level of the Church, no longer pretending to be the receiver of the divine.

But, as in everything, there is a lighter side to Pisces that we may now lose also – an honoring of the invisible realm and a willingness to trust something other than the human ego. In the ages to come we may lose this sense of awe in the face of mystery if science becomes too arrogant with its own knowledge.

Nostradamus was also very choosy about the words he employed in each of the verses he wrote. The French word "verbe" has been taken to mean "word" in English. But Nostradamus was aware of the process of changing life. He would have understood that the years before the end of the 20th century were years of movement. Life is a verb rather than

The ancient rites of pagan cults such as the Celtic Druids have returned to us from the distant past, to become of fascination again to a humanity sadly disillusioned by the organized religions, which seem only to bring suffering and war.

a noun. We are in a constant state of change. We are divine verbs. That divine movement, us, gives to life (the substance) that which contains the sky and the land (heaven and earth). We human beings, ever changing, contain both heaven (God) and Earth (humanity). We are the "occult gold to the mystic deed."

"Body, soul and mind are all powerful."

The Aquarian Age has brought an awareness of the connections between the body, the soul, and the mind. There are even festivals and exhibitions throughout the world devoted to these connections. One cannot live and thrive without the others. We are one force – body, mind, and soul. And more than this, as God moves down from his throne upon the clouds to a place in our individual hearts, so we, each of us, become all powerful. This is not intended to reflect on power in a political sense, but power of the individual to decide his or her own fate. Nostradamus, in effect, saw the changes that would occur during the latter years of this century – the power that would bring religion into the hearts of man.

"All is beneath his feet, like the seat of the heavens."

In effect, what the prophecy states is that man would learn to turn hell on Earth into heaven on Earth and have dominion over both.

Now all this may sound unlikely if you are looking out from the perspective of war, scandal, hatred, and disaster, but the very basis of the Aquarian Age gives clear indications that once the poison inherent in society is cleaned out, change will be for the better.

The Gift of Prometheus

Above ~ *The gift of the power to make our lives work brings the greatest responsibility. Nobody is going to do it for us – no God, no outside power, only us. A banner hung on Nelson's column in Trafalgar Square, protesting against the results of the UNCED conference in Rio, illustrates current dissatisfaction with the methods being used to "cure" the world of its man-imposed ills. Economy still dominates nature.*

P ROMETHEUS TOOK FIRE FROM THE GODS and gave it to man. In effect, this is what is happening to mankind today. We are receiving the powers that were originally supposed to be allocated to God, and we are finding ourselves capable of exercising them. In areas such as genetic engineering, where scientists are actually able to create life, we are faced by moral and religious dilemmas that would once have been settled by the Church tied to a stake and set by fire. Do we dare to presume that we are able to make life, change life, create the universe around us?

Nostradamus and the Aquarian Age state very clearly that we are.

"All is beneath his feet, like the seat of the heavens." Everything that was once the realm of heaven is now the realm of mankind, bringing with it the same responsibilities.

All this fits neatly together with what we have already seen – the Aquarian power to cooperate with life and nature. Religiousness, too, is a cooperation with God, and the responsibility to make it work to our benefit rests solely with this partnership.

"The divine verb will give to the substance that which contains the sky and the land (heaven and earth), occult gold to the mystic deed."

Nostradamus so eloquently encapsulates the whole of this concept within so few words.

"Occult gold to the mystic deed" forms perhaps the most significant aspect of all the words of the verse. Occult gold was that which came into being once the alchemical process had been fulfilled. The base metal of humanity, untried, unsophisticated, undeveloped, was subjected to the alchemical processes of the magician and turned into gold. The mystic deed is the power of God. So mankind turns himself from base metal into gold through understanding God. In the chapter devoted to Nostradamus' vision of how religion will change, we will examine how this transformation might occur.

On this page ~ *Prometheus Bound. Prometheus was the Greek god of fire, and maker of man. In stealing the fire from Zeus and returning it to Earth, Prometheus's gift has always been seen as the ultimate ability to make human life.*

In our history and our science there has never been any question of humans being able to create life itself, except through the natural processes of reproduction. Beyond the fiction of Frankenstein, we have not had to face such a gift before.

But during the latter years of the 20th century, and the early years of the 21st century that is changing and will change still further. We have already found ways of altering the genetic structure of unborn foetuses, and we can skillfully alter the structure of animal and plant life. What will come next as the gift of Prometheus is handed to us?

Will be continue to erect statues ot legal murderers rather than listen to the cries of the starving? Will we continue to send rockets to other planets, while this one is falling from the skies?

Nostradamus tells us that during these last millennial years we will finally begin to see the light.

This look at the broadest element of astrology forms our basis for the next fifty years of mankind's world changes, and we will see in the rest of the book how these vital changes transform the planet Earth from the muddle and chaos it is in at present into a more ordered and beautiful place for the future and the Aquarian Age itself.

Before we move into the particular subjects of Nostradamus' prophecies, we have one further astrological indication to help us see the overall trend.

The Cusp of Chaos

"Somewhere where the climate is opposite to Babylon, there will be a great blood-letting. Land, sea, air and sky (heaven) will seem unjust. Sects, hunger, reigns, pestilences confusion."

IF WE LOOK BACK over the greater part of the 20th century, casting our eyes, over the newspaper headlines of the 1900s, virtually all we see is chaos and confusion. Following World War I we read of almost continuous upheaval with nations collapsing, leaders assassinated, diseases rampant, wars almost continuous, religions falling apart, crime increasing. We seem only just to survive in an age of complete pandemonium.

In the 1990s we still hear of the same stories: struggles in Yugoslavia, increased drug traffic in Europe and the United States, the destruction of the rain forests, the starvation of the peoples of the Baltic Countries, and the rapid destruction of Africa through AIDS. This is the "blood-letting," seen by a doctor who watched his colleagues bleed their patients – the letting out of poisons that accompanies the cusp of the Aquarian Age and the transit of Pluto through Scorpio. And although the transit is completed around 1997-8, the chaos of the Aquarian cusp will continue into the 21st century.

Our age is not unique in its astonishing chaos, but we are unique in our ability to broadcast our troubles instantly to the rest of the world, and we have perhaps nastier weapons and a far greater capacity to destroy ourselves.

When a body is about to die it kicks violently: the last vibrations, the rattle of death. Before any major transformation and rebirth can take place, the Earth and its people must detoxify themselves. Virtually the whole of the 20th century, the last 100 years of this millennium and the lead up to the Aquarian Age can be seen as the death rattle of the age of unreason. We are entering a new age, and the chaos we experience on a day-to-day level is the death of the old age.

During the 1980s and early 1990s we have been experiencing this transit of Pluto through the sign of Scorpio, something that occurs approximately every 248 years as Pluto passes through the various signs in an elliptical orbit. This previously occurred at the end of the 15th century,

We live in a cusp of chaos, and the chaos will continue for some years, at least until the end of the century/millennium. We are told that the Los Angeles riots of 1992 will be repeated with greater violence yet, and that we still face the biggest ever earthquakes in that area of the world.

Chaos reigns – a typical scene in Sarajevo during 1992, the center of a civil war which threatens the whole of Europe.

coinciding with the advent of the Renaissance, the collapse of the Byzantium Empire, and the rise of the Muslim world. Here began the Inquisition, the discovery of the New World and the arrival of the dreaded disease syphilis into western Europe.

This transit was just completed by the time of Nostradamus' birth. In his epistle to the French King Henry II, Nostradamus makes a direct reference to the effects of this transit, although in fact he would not have been aware of the planet Pluto as it was not discovered until well after his death.

"Then the impurities and abominations will be brought to the surface and made manifest...toward the end of a change in reign" (possibly between Elizabeth II and Charles). Pluto in transit through Scorpio, in astrological terms, indicates the cleansing of everything that is old, worn out, dead, and rotten to prepare the ground for fresh growth. Its central feature is the exposure of corruption, something that seems eminently appropriate to the 1980s and 1990s with so many financial and political scandals occupying our newspaper headlines. Nostradamus said it in his own way: "Land, sea, air and sky (heaven) will seem unjust." Everything everywhere, even heaven, will seem to be unjust, or unjustified.

It is incidentally interesting to note that the heir to the British throne, Prince Charles, is currently most vulnerable to this influence as his sign is Scorpio and the present transit of Pluto is on his Sun in Scorpio, thus reflecting profound change and disruption in his personal life continuing through 1995. All secrets float to the surface and what makes it all the worse is that it is occurring at the same time as the cusp change between the broader ages of Pisces and Aquarius, where anxiety and fear is already rife. So the mix is pretty potent and the result very difficult.

The transit of the planet Pluto occurs through the sign of Scorpio, between 1980 and 1997-8. It is fascinating to note just how the progress of the planets in transition have affected our "life-discoveries," for before Pluto passed through Scorpio it transited Libra, thus reflecting deep changes in our ideas about marriage, love, and human relationships. Initially, this came with idealism, the "free-love" of the 60s, including easy divorce, early communal living, and sexual equality. Then Pluto moved into Scorpio and we found out just how much rot there was beneath the surface in every walk of life due to the darker side of human nature. The idealism of the 1960s led us straight into our own secret corruption and power games. The next stage occurs when Pluto enters Sagittarius, and then we will be asking what it has all been about, how can we become better after all this detoxification.

Earth Talk

O NE OF THE MOST PROMINENT AREAS that Scorpio influences is shared resources; anything to do with facilities or sources of energy that we all share together. We will therefore continue to see Pluto's detoxification impact in relation to our environment. Pluto, in effect, has been talking to planet Earth, as she passes by en route for Sagittarius. This transit through Scorpio therefore is helping us to bring the poisons of our past, thoughtless work to the surface. We have spent almost 300 years burning up nature's shared resources to fuel our rush to industrial growth. For what? To watch the beauty of nature and life deteriorate and die, to watch animal life become extinct, and to watch human beings die in their millions from the poisons that have resulted, to say nothing of the killing of the planet's breathing trees.

And this sweating out of global poisons will continue almost to the end of this decade before other areas of life are touched by Pluto's passing. This is the dark side of the use of material resources.

Left ~ *Nostradamus speaks of the purification which the Earth and its people will undergo during the last years of this century. Pluto's transit through the heavens acts as a kind of "house cleaner," exposing and detoxifying everything in its path. Mother Earth herself responds to Pluto's cleansing action with natural disasters such as hurricane "Hugo" which caused havoc in Puerto Rico on September 21, 1989. There will be much more of this, for we are intimately connected to our planet. In effect we ARE our planet, so that as we shed our poisons, so does She.*

Body Talk

T HE EQUALLY DARK SIDE of the use of human resources is another aspect of Pluto's passing through Scorpio, that of Scorpio's other major influence, human sexuality and its detoxification through disease.

When Pluto passed through the sign of Scorpio during the late years of the 15th century, syphilis was born. The story says that during the reign of Charles VIII of France, when he invaded Italy, the Italians maintained that the French soldiers brought the disease with them, and the French maintained that they got it from the Italians.

In our 20th century version of this same astrological concurrence we have discovered AIDS (though it must also be said that syphilis is still very much alive). In this way Scorpio and Pluto have joined hands to change the old rules that govern sex and relationships. Because of AIDS, many feelings like love, guilt, fear, passion, prejudice, and power have come into question. It is no longer safe to have sexual contact with anyone unless a conscious effort has been made to secure the parties against death. And the indications are that the situation will worsen before it gets better. Sex and death have never joined hands quite to this extent before.

So during this age, the transits are about as vital as any could be.

The Character of Scorpio

 LTHOUGH THIS MAY SEEM to be all doom and despondency, as very often Nostradamus manages to be, there is an underlying positive purpose that can be seen between the lines of both the prophet's words and the astrological tendencies.

The whole process of relationships, for example, has been brought into question, not only from the point of view of the risk of sexually transmitted diseases, but from the point of view of moral and religious standards. Marriage has become highly questionable as a contractual process between human beings, bringing them together into something that cannot be written down and signed off. Love doesn't necessarily flourish under these conditions. On the other hand, with the threat of AIDS, many people are feeling that the only potentially safe route is to stay with one person throughout life. At least this way we may have a chance of staying alive. So here again we have great confusion.

Feminism has also brought many new rules to relationships, as well as new prejudices, and attitudes. Men can now express their "feminine" side as well as their masculine. Women are experiencing areas of life that

Of all the signs that will be transited by Pluto's clean-up, Scorpio is the most potent, as it relates to sexual behavior. The spread of the AIDS virus in recent years is profoundly influencing our attitudes towards sexuality, and provoking ever deeper levels of discussion and examination of this part of our lives. Nostradamus tells us that we are all connected in this world and the passing of Pluto will give us the opportunity to live happier times in the future.
Left *~ The Egyptian Scorpion Goddess, Selket.*

were once the sole domain of the male. But there are also angry elements to feminism that have caused the pendulum to swing as Pluto and Scorpio pass. It is interesting to note the backlash that occurred in America in the 1992 election as the Republican party became the anti-abortion party, subtly suggesting that women should get "back into the kitchen." This kind of side-effect that grows out of the sexual "melting pot" that is being so vigorously stirred during the 1990s, illustrates the human tendency to avoid dealing with new responsibilities and insights in favor of retreating into the old sets of attitudes.

Everything is changing, and this process of change at its basis, is one that gives us the opportunity to find new roles, new attitudes towards each other, so that perhaps there is something new to come out of the negative that will produce greater happiness in the future.

Once we have abandoned our desire to retreat into the old ways of life: family, marriage, nation etc., once we have faced the possibility that perhaps these ways have ceased to work effectively, perhaps then something fresh will surface behind the toxins. The story can be seen in all matters of life today.

Toward Cooperative Freedom

We have watched, in every living room of the world, the death of communism in the old Soviet Union, and scenes such as the one on this page, where a statue of Lenin is removed from a Berlin square.

But the immediate result of this "blood-letting" which creates such dramatic changes in history, is not immediately more freedom. First there is a tendency in human nature to rush for cover, to withdraw into a kind of tribal insecurity.

Countries try to re-establish their borders, languages are jealously maintained, and life appears to be reducing, less cooperative than before. But this is only a stage in the evolution of major change, which eventually, during the early years of the 21st century, will see a more positive world.

"Somewhere where the climate is opposite to Babylon, there will be a great blood-letting."

S ALWAYS, Nostradamus uses specific events to get a story started. The likely place that has a "climate opposite to Babylon" is almost certainly the Soviet Union. The "great blood-letting" must be understood in the light of how the process of blood-letting was employed in Nostradamus' day. Everything that related to disease during the period of the 16th century was believed to be caused by toxins in the body. Very apt in terms of our astrological context. The medical methods were very simple. An arm or leg was either cut and blood dripped (or flooded) from the body, or leeches were used to suck the blood from the poor unfortunate sufferer. In this way it was believed that poisons circulating in the body would flow out with the "bad blood."

We use the term "bad blood" even today, especially to describe a situation where people are in conflict. In those bad old days, doctors believed that the body was in a kind of conflict with itself.

So "blood-letting" in the context of this country with the climate opposite to Babylon, may be seen as the detoxification of Communism – letting the poisons of the old repressed social structure run out of the veins of the former Soviet Union.

We know now that the death of Communism released an extraordinary flood of poisons into the world. All the communist countries were forced into re-examining their most intimate secrets. A vast sector of the world's population was suddenly free. But free to do what?

"Land, sea, air and sky (heaven) will seem unjust."

Everything was without justice, and the most natural result of such a freedom is both revolution and withdrawal. We have seen this most potently within the countries of what was Yugoslavia, where fear and deep anxiety engendered over decades have led to a furious response of tribal withdrawal.

We saw the anger in Romania, in Albania, and may still see more of it in the parts of the Soviet Union that have yet to bring their anger to the surface.

"Sects, famine, kingdoms, plagues, confusion."

Nostradamus sums up the whole story in one short line. "Sects, famine, kingdoms, plagues, confusion". Except that he is not satisfied simply to bring us the story of unrest in national areas. He links it also to religion and confusion. And this brings us smartly back to our Aquarian Age and the detoxification of Pluto passing through Scorpio on its way to Sagittarius.

As the anxiety for change begins to settle down, as the European Community begins to work out its new roles and models, as the Yugoslavian countries begin to work out their differences, so the Aquarian Age will have its way. But cooperation will follow, and with it some measure of peace and prosperity.

Toward the middle of the next century – around 2050 – according to both Nostradamus and the relevant astrological readings, this will have reached at least the stage of "outline planning permission." But there is another area that will also come under the hammer of the cusp of chaos and the influence of the planet Pluto, and that resides within the characteristic of Sagittarius.

A New God ~ Private Matters & Meditation

E HAVE ALREADY, earlier in this chapter, spoken of the influence of the Aquarian Age over our organized religions. This is the broad view. But there is still more influence that will cause changes to occur within the religions of the near future.

Pluto, within the context of the Aquarian Age, moves away from influencing Scorpio and into influencing Sagittarius around the last years of the 20th century and the first years of the next millennium. It is almost as though Pluto is a conscientious house cleaner, disinfecting and cleaning each particular area of human life on its route through the skies. For Sagittarius and Pluto combined bring into sharp relief the poisons and failings of religious dogma. As if the process was not already bad enough with the upheaval taking place within the hallowed walls of Catholicism.

Very soon, according to Nostradamus in many of his quatrains, there is more to come. In fact, effectively virtually all of the values of organized religion will have to change under this powerful aspect.

"Sects, famine, kingdoms, plagues, confusion."

During the Piscean Age there was less questioning of God. But now everyone is doubting those poor fellows that are supposed to be the emissaries of God. One of the most common results of disillusionment in established religion is the increased emergence of religious sects, of which there have been many in the latter half of this century. And Nostradamus spins out his line like a cleverly fashioned decoration, each

As Pluto passes from Scorpio into the Sagittarius, its influence begins to be felt in religious areas of life. During the early years of the 1990s we already began to feel its effects, as the organized religions started to undergo changes that threaten their very fabric. This upheaval will continue through to the end of the millennium and beyond.

end supported by a question and answer – an answer and a question. "Sects" at one end, and "confusion" at the other. What better poles to support the line in the middle of "famine, kingdoms and plagues"?

Some readers will have heard of the teacher J.Krishnamurti, who attracted a strong, widespread following with his message of freedom and love. More especially, the readers of the previous books in this series will have heard of the Master, Osho Rajneesh, whose people are still spreading a new message of religiousness and meditation from their ashram in India. And there are many more new religious leaders to whom we could point as examples of fresh approaches to God that are of popular value during this century.

However, there seems to be a whole new route to the new God, as we will see in the chapter in this book devoted to the subject. But there is one underlying theme – that God is becoming private and personal, available to everyone, not as an all powerful god living in some distant heaven, but rather a god that resides inside all of us. There are probably more quatrains, as we shall see, related to this theme than almost any other in Nostradamus' works.

Above ~ The Sacred dances of the Russian spiritual master George Gurdjieff being performed at the Osho Commune International in India, where new life is breathed into ancient and sacred rites. During the last years of the '20th century we will see more and more interest in the more subtle and personal religious understanding of life's mysteries.

And so, we have touched on the very broadest foundations for our future changes. We have seen something of the cusp of the Aquarian Age that occupies the zodiac in the present and future years, and we have touched upon the "clean-up" process exacted by Pluto in Scorpio and Sagittarius. These are the building blocks that Nostradamus actually used, both through his knowledge of astrology and his psychic powers, for the rationalization of his predictions.

A Taste of Joy to come

WE CAN, AS A FINAL LEAD IN to the actual predictions, take a passing and brief look at the last 40 years of our present millennium, as these will become highly significant as we get further into Nostradamus' work. They are years of both continuing difficulties but also increasingly positive trends towards rebuilding our world and ourselves in a better way.

Les fleurs (fleaux) passes diminue le monde,
Long temps la paix terres inhabitees:
Seur marchera par ciel, serre, mer & onde:
Puis de nouveau les guerres suscitees.
C1 63

"Flowers (or pestilences) passed, reduces the world, for a long time peace inhabits the lands: people will travel through and embrace the sky, sea and land: then wars will start up again."

Nostradamus starts this verse with a double-meaning. The word "fleurs" in modern French means flower, while the old Provence word "fleaux" means pestilence or disease. Dr. Michel de Nostradame would cure the dreaded bubonic plague by gathering rose petals by the thousands, drying them and crushing them, then putting them in simple capsules to be placed beneath the tongue of the plague sufferer. The time release of rose petals provided vitamin C and helped cure the disease.

The connection between flowers and disease was an intimate one for Nostradamus and this leads us into this particular verse.

"Flowers (or pestilences) passed, reduces the world,"

We can quickly date the prediction by looking at the line which reads:

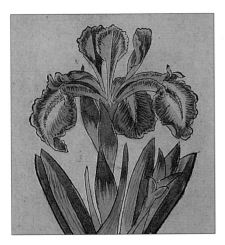

Top left ~ *Rosa muscosa, the moss rose.*
Left ~ *"The Madonna of the rose bower" – by Martin Schongauer, 1473, found in the church of Saint Martin, Colmar, France. The rose is depicted here as a religious symbol, a kind of adjunct to sanctity, as well as a symbol of virtue. At the same time, Nostradamus was using rose petals for curing the plague. Thus, religion and nature, science and love come together in the flower.*
Above ~ *the Iris, this illustration taken from a book entitled "La Clef des Champs" by Jacques le Moyne de Morgues. Nostradamus employed many flowers as part of his 16th-century homeopathic cures, already well in advance of his times.*

"people will travel through and embrace the sky, sea and land." This indication of a time when we became familiar with all forms of travel, together with other clues in the verse, points to the 1960s. Nostradamus' reference to the flowers (or flower-power) of the 1960s, a delicate power to heal mankind after the terrors of the World Wars, confirms the timing. The 1960s were a significant time in our evolution for they brought to the surface the idea that life was not all death and destruction, that the madness of the two World Wars was perhaps merely a foul sore on the surface of mankind and could be passed by in favor of better things.

The 1960s diminished the world in size by bringing mankind together for a short time in a kind of innocent expression of creativity, at least in the "civilized" western world of the time. Music, art, and a kind of rebelious design, particularly in fashion, dominated this unique decade. There was also a tinge of Eastern beauty catalyzed by the popular musicians of the day. Riches came from music and make-up. The interesting people were the photographers and fashion models, the actors and hippies.

The people of the 1960s weren't yet aware of what the "Atom bomb" had really done, what pollution would mean, what a disgusting world was being created. They were too busy watching everything beautiful.

It was a foretaste, according to Nostradamus, of what would come again much later, a time that we have not yet reached in the 1990s.

In addition, there was a most interesting and unusual planetary conjunction in the heavens of the 1960s, a Uranus/Pluto conjunction in Virgo, the sign of daily life, natural law, and the cycles of nature. This conjunction reflected a period of radical change in thinking about the quality of daily life and certainly can be tied in with the whole concept of "flower-power."

What comes out of this conjunction is, of course, people – those people born in the 1960s within that conjunction. During the 1990s and into the next century, these people reach their 30s and 40s, a time when they begin to influence the world most profoundly, in positions of responsibility within society. The vision of the 1960s may have passed

Days gone by – the 60s – still carry a strong influence at the end of the century. Most of those in the picture are world famous today – John Lennon (whose influence still lingers long after his death), Paul McCartney, Mia Farrow, George Harrison, Donovan. The impact of their creative, eccentric, and often revolutionary behavior is still being felt.

by ("Where are they now?"), and many people may have "sold out" to become regular members of the social order. But those born in that conjunction still carry the same vision within them. They are embodiments of it, and still better they have learned the more realistic ecological consciousness that has developed since the 1960s flower-power generation that gave them life. We may see these people provide an important influence in the Virgo spheres of Earth consciousness in the last years of the 20th century and the first decade of the 21st century.

"...for a long time peace inhabits the lands..."

The way Nostradamus writes this poetic verses brings the tone of what he saw of our lives in the 20th century. "Flowers (or pestilences) passed, reduces the world, for a long time peace inhabits the lands: people will travel through and embrace the sky, sea, and land.." We can almost feel what he meant. When nations are less important than love and harmony, so the world gets smaller. When the pestilences of life are passed, so we come together as one world. This in turn brings peace. And with peace people can afford to embrace the land. This was the way of the 1960s, the way of innocence, and it formulated the beginning of a transformative process, underpinned by the larger shift into Aquarius, that is essentially healing particularly in relation to our connections with the Earth and our ability to integrate physical and psychic life.

The great conjunction of Uranus and Neptune in Capricorn during the

61

1990s, is forming a trine (a positive aspect) to the earlier Uranus/Pluto conjunction in Virgo during the 1960s, thus suggesting that even though we are still in a terrible mess, some healing process is being accelerated during the last years of the 20th century. Put another way, the 1990s effectively form a kind of positive echo of the 1960s. The Uranus/Pluto conjunction during the 1960s marked a period of significant upheaval with new and far-reaching ideas emerging from the collective unconscious. This period can, in effect, therefore form a kind of astrological "birth chart" for us to work forward from. Any transiting planets during the last decade of the millennium that hit that "birth" conjunction of Uranus/Pluto will activate its meaning and the effects within the collective psyche.

During the Uranus and Neptune conjunction in Capricorn of the 1990s, the trine (120-degree angle) or harmonious aspect, to the original conjunction in the 1960s "birth chart" effectively stirs it up all over again, as though we were going through something very similar to the 1960s in social, political and religious unrest, upheaval and change. But because the aspect is harmonious, it means that the original energy is likely to be expressed in positive ways that provide resolutions to the problems that arose in the 1960s, resulting in positive and creative changes. This is the driving force that pushes the poisons to the surface, a positive force that will bring us quite soon out of the apparent chaos.

"..then wars will start up again."

And of course he was right about this. In fact, after the 1960s we faced a mass psychosis on almost every level, indeed on a collective level, and this has continued right through into the 1990s.

Radical change on this level means more than just a muddled existence. It is either breakdown or breakthrough that we are facing. If we look back at some of the other prophets aside from Nostradamus, we find constantly concurring visions that have mostly been interpreted as applying to the last decade of the 20th century.

The 60s formed an astrological birth chart, a kind of new order which provided the future with many different kinds of behavior, many new attitudes. In the 90s we face either breakdown or breakthrough as a result of these radical changes, changes that are accompanied by a detoxification of the whole of society.

APPLE FILMS present ·
A KING FEATURES PRODUCTION
THE BEATLES
"YELLOW SUBMARINE" U
starring
SGT. PEPPER'S LONELY HEARTS CLUB BAND
Design · HEINZ EIDELMANN
Produced by AL BRODAX · Directed by GEORGE DUNNING
COLOUR by DeLuxe   United Artists

KING FEATURES—SUBAFILMS LTD. 1968

We will see the 60s repeated, perhaps in a slightly different form, but nevertheless a kind of new "flower-power" is emerging during the last years of the 20th century, to blossom in the next millennium. However cliched it may sound now, the understanding and application of love within society will change everything in our future.

From Gautama the Buddha we can read in the *Diamond Sutra* that he claimed that with each 25 centuries there comes a radical change of consciousness on Earth with an accompanying period of intense chaos. A great Master such as Buddha would come to humanity only when the "Wheel of Dharma" needed a push. The "wheel" was seen in Eastern tradition as a force of energy that shifted the progress of the world on a massive scale. In astrological terms it is known as "The Great Year," a concept familiar to Nostradamus. Just before the wheel was pushed again there would inevitably be a period of "the dark night of the soul," in which the world went through a cleansing.

The last push of the wheel was 25 centuries ago, and it has now slowed down and come to rest as the Buddha's age dies. According to the Buddhist concept, we are due for another big push.

John of Patmos, the man who was responsible for the *Book of Revelations* in the *Bible*, had a massive apocalyptic vision in which he witnessed a millennium of peace and a new spirituality with a new Adam who would appear in our age. "And I saw a new Heaven and a new Earth; for the first Heaven and the first Earth were passed away."

D.H.Lawrence, in his book on Revelations gives us his interpretation:
"The famous book of seven seals in this place is the body of man. Of man; of Adam; of any man... And the seven seals are the seven centers or gates of his dynamic consciousness. We are witnessing the opening and conquest of the great psychic centers of the human body. The old Adam is going to be conquered, die and be reborn as the new Adam. But in stages. In seven stages, or six stages and then a climax, seven."

The prophet Merlin, the wizard and mystic sage who taught the legendary King Arthur in ancient Britain, the instigator of the quest for the Holy Grail, left a book of prophecies, and in it verse 88 describes our time:
"Root and branch shall change places and the newness of the thing shall pass as a miracle."

In the Native American world we hear the same story from the Hopi:

*Peace marches and protests, sit-ins
and constant intellectual revolutions
will continue through these coming
years. The youth revolution began in
the 60s and has not ceased in the
following three decades. New
rebellious organizations such as
Greenpeace have grown up during
the 1980s and 1990s, to hound the
consciences of industry and state,
making their point very clear with
actions that speak louder than words.
We are in transition, both at ground-
level in human behavior, and in the
astrological skies.*

*"The emergence of the future fifth world has begun. You can read
this in the earth itself. Plant-forms from previous worlds have begun
to spring up as seeds...the same kinds of seeds are being planted in
the sky as stars. The same kinds of seeds are being planted in our
hearts. All these are the same, depending on how you look at them.
This is what makes the emergence to the next, fifth world."*

And of course the prophet who is the subject of this book also spoke
of "a thousand years of peace...when the seventh millennium has
come..."

In his book *Unknown Man* (1988, Simon & Schuster), the author Yatri
speaks of an evolutionary transition that mankind undertakes in his
stages of growth on a global level. The basis of his theory is that we have
to sustain a period of disaster and chaos before we can be pitched forward into a new world order.

We are clearly at the center of just such a period now.

So we have seen the wars start up again that Nostradamus predicted.
And the result may be breakdown or breakthrough. But as the author
hopes to show in the pages of this book, the transformation will be
brought about by us all. The next push of the Wheel of Dharma will not
be given by any single individual, but by everyone.

Chapter 2
NEW WORLDS

Our time in this century, if observed from 400 years ago, would certainly look like a holocaust. **Below** *~ The Gulf War of 1990-1991: British troops move through the Saudi Arabian desert.* **Opposite** *~ the US Marines 3rd Attack Battalion in Saudi Arabia. One of the most extraordinary aspects of the Gulf War was the ability of the Western powers to move massive quantities of armaments across great distances, in a matter of days.*

"**B**UT MY SON, lest I venture too far for your future perception, be aware that men of letters shall make grand and usually boastful claims about the way I interpreted the world, before the worldwide conflagration that is to bring so many catastrophes and such revolutions that scarcely any lands will not be covered by water, and this will last until all has perished save history and geography themselves. This is why, before and after these revolutions in various countries, the rains will be so diminished and such abundance of fire and fiery missiles shall fall from the heavens that nothing shall escape the holocaust. And this will occur before the last conflagration. For before war ends the century and in its final stages it will hold the century under its sway. Some countries will be in the grip of revolution for several years, and others ruined for still longer period. And now that we are in a republican era, with Almighty God's aid, and before completing its full cycle, the monarchy will return, then the Golden Age. For according to the celestial signs, the Golden Age shall return, and after all calculations, with the world near to an all-encompassing revolution – from the time of writing 177 years 3 months 11 days – plague, long famine and wars, and still more floods from now until the stated time. Before and after these humanity shall several times be so severely diminished that scarcely anyone shall be found who wishes to take over the fields, which shall become free where they had previously been tied. This will be after the visible judgment of heaven, before we reach the millennium which shall complete all."

Nostradamus' *Preface to his son César*, Salon 1st March, 1555.

Doomsday Fears

E BEGIN THIS CHAPTER with a section from Nostradamus' preface to his son, probably the most daring piece of prophecy anywhere in the history of mankind. But before we become too involved in the details and time-spans provided in this passage, we should bring an important matter to the surface.

Nostradamus lived in a period of history that was essentially local. As we hinted at the very beginning of the book, speeds of communication were only as fast as the fastest set of four legs available. Neighborhoods were, for most people, the total scope of the universe. People traveled by donkey to the market in the nearby village and sold their goods. A noble or person of high station might occasionally visit the capital city of the country.

Wars were fought on hillsides to conquer towns or castles. Death in battle came from a sword, an arrow, or at worst from a metal ball fired from a musket. There was no technology in the way that we know it in the 20th century, and certainly no rockets or missiles.

For a man living in such times to be suddenly thrust forward four centuries and more into the future, the 20th century would look like a global insane asylum.

In a matter of weeks during the 1991 Gulf War, an entire army of thousands of huge rolling tanks, aircraft, massive ships, each one the size of a medieval village, and hundreds of thousands of men were physically transported from the United States and allied countries to the Middle East.

Left ~ the storming of the Bastille.
Below ~ examples of modern warfare in Kuwait.
The battles during Nostradamus' lifetime were
fought locally, on the side of a hill or within a
single town. Today, war is global and massive.
From his viewpoint the difference between then and
now would have looked like the difference between
a small skirmish and the end of the world.
It is not surprising, therefore, that the prophet's
predictions have such an atmosphere of doom and
gloom in relation to our times.

This is a distance of several thousand miles. This would be equivalent
to suggesting to Nostradamus that he arrange to transport the entire population of Paris plus all the carriages, several streets including the houses,
and all the French navy to the New World just discovered by Columbus
— literally an impossible task.

If we believe in his abilities as a prophet, Nostradamus was watching the Gulf War, the Vietnam War, the World Wars, and all of the other
atrocities perpetrated by mankind in the past years of this century, and
would clearly have imagined that he was seeing a blazing holocaust of
madness. In effect, as a seer of the future, he must have experienced this
century's insanities, en masse, as one major holocaust. Given this perspective, he could be forgiven for thinking that 20th century man had
reached the pinnacle of his idiocy, that, "... such abundance of fire and
fiery missiles shall fall from the heavens that nothing shall escape the
holocaust."

Why not? It's true. Nothing has escaped the holocaust. We are all
involved in it.

Modern interpreters of Nostradamus make the mistake of imagining
that it can get worse. They tend not to understand that it is already as
bad as it can be. This is not to say that the "holocaust" will not continue
for some years yet, but to Nostradamus, "For before war ends the century and in its final stages it will hold the century under its sway. Some
countries will be in the grip of revolution for several years, and others
ruined for still longer period." This is it. We are in the holocaust now.

Nostradamus timed the beginning of the French Revolution from the day when Jean Jacques Rousseau entered Paris with his concepts of rule by the people. The prophet's astonishing predictions range from this date through to our present time where revolutions are happening all over the world every year. Here begins our story for the future.

Rousseau & Revolution

"...from the time of writing 177 years 3 months 11 days – plague, long famine and wars, and still more floods from now until the stated time."

NOSTRADAMUS WROTE THIS astonishing piece of prediction on 1 March, 1555. 177 years, 3 months, and 11 days after that date brings us to 24 June, 1732 taking into account the changes in calendar reckoning. This happens to be the exact date that Jean-Jacques Rousseau went to Paris for the first time and, from Nostradamus' view point, began the path that would lead to atheism and revolution throughout the Western world, starting with the French Revolution in 1792.

This is such an astonishing piece of prophetic daring that one is almost breathless at the scope of it. What the prophet is telling us is that from his own time until the year 1732 there will be: "...plague, long famine and wars, and still more floods from now until the stated time." Then, from Rousseau's time until the end of the millennium we shall see that, "...humanity shall several times be so severely diminished that scarcely anyone shall be found who wishes to take over the fields, which shall become free where they had previously been tied."

And finally, "This will be after the visible judgment of heaven, before we reach the millennium which shall complete all."

What we see from this mapping of his future and our past and present, is a period of history that began the last stages of the Christian era, the end of the Piscean Age. By 1732 the planets were moving into the cusp of the Piscean and Aquarian Age, and by 1999 we will be almost fully into the next era, as we have discussed, the Aquarian Age. Nostradamus saw this most clearly as a period of huge adjustment including famines, wars, plagues and holocaust-like behavior right at the end in the last few decades of this millennium.

In some ways, the interpretations that have suggested we will all go up in flames at the end of this millennium might have been more dramatic, but in reality the truer picture is that the flames are already burning. Let us start mapping the scenario for the future with perhaps the single most popular quatrain of all.

Mabus The Painter

1960 ~ 2000 ~ THE HOLOCAUST

Mabus puis tost alors mourra, viendra
De gens et bête une horrible défaite:
Puis tout à coup la vengeance on verra,
Cent, main, soif, faim quand courra la comète.

"Mabus then will soon die, there will come a horrible defeat for people and animals:
then suddenly one will see vengeance, hundred, hand, thirst, hunger when the comet will run."

He strides from the mountains,
he stands near the pines,
We saw it: He changes the water to wines,
His voice can evoke the departed!

If only you heard how I laugh in the dark!
My hour has come, now the quarry is snared,
Now fish fill the nets with their swarming.

The mob is afoot, both the foolish and wise,
They crash through the cornfields and tear up the trees,
Make way for the train of the Risen!

The sky has no marvels I cannot confer,
A hairsbreadth amiss, but you do not discern
The hoax, for your senses are blunted.

The facile I bring for the labored and rare,

Make something like gold out of clay, or a sham
Like juice full of fragrance and spices.

And what the great prophet eschewed I have taught:
The art without clearing or sowing or toil
To live on the stores of the furrow.

The lord of all vermin extends his domains,
No treasure escapes him, his joys never wane.
And down with the rest, with the rebels!

You cheer, you are charmed by demoniac ruse,
Exhaust the old honeys, and only when doom
Approaches you will feel you are beggared,

And hang out your tongues, but the bucket is dry.
They flounder like cows when the barn is afire –
And grimly the trumpet is sounded!

The Antichrist by Stefan George
(Translated by Olga Marx and Ernst Morwitz, with doctoring by Richard Leigh)

The man depicted on the previous page was painted by the Dutch artist Mabuse, who lived during Nostradamus' lifetime. The word Mabus in the prophet's verses has always been taken to be the third antichrist by interpreters, but there is a far more convincing explanation available on these pages.

THE QUATRAIN AT THE BEGINNING OF THIS SECTION is one of the most significant verses within the whole of Nostradamus' predictions, particularly so for those who look forward to the coming of the "Antichrist" (seen still by the best known interpreters as likely to be a single individual) and the final holocaust due, according to modern commentaries, at the end of this century. On these pages also, is a powerful poetic representation of the concept of the Antichrist, that expresses better than any explanation or definition the human fears of a single, ghastly individual with black and divine powers that will one day destroy us all.

As we discussed earlier in this chapter, the more realistic view, though one that may be disappointing to some, is that we are the holocaust. We began our current quest to aid the destruction of humanity with World War I and we have been continuing in this vein almost without stop ever since. So what is this "Antichrist?" Is there another explanation for "Mabus?"

Interpreters have suggested that there are at least three key words within the quatrains that indicate the presence of three individuals during mankind's recent history, that are the worst three individual humans ever to stand on the planet earth. The first was Napoleon, who ruled France and was the perpetrator of terrible wars and the destruction of many hundreds of thousands of people. One of Nostradamus' quatrains contains three words, "PAU, NAY, OLORON," at the beginning of the first line of the quatrain and in the first quatrain of a "Century", where often his most dramatic verses appear. Interpreters have supposed this to be an anagram of the name Napoleon Roy or King Napoleon.

Here is said to be Antichrist number one.

The second horror is taken to be Hitler, and certainly there are a number of interesting quatrains that refer to a "Hister" or "Ister" as our contending Antichrist number two.

There is, however, nothing conclusive about any of this, except that

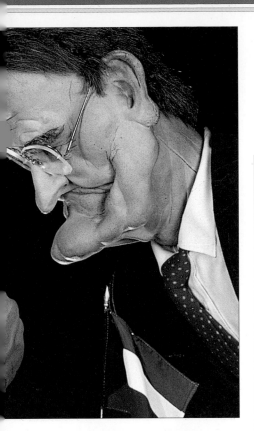

we do have these two characters in our past upon whom to pin the labels that Nostradamus gave us.

As to the third Antichrist, we have no such luxury, though there have been a few possible contenders such as Khomeini, Gaddafi, and Hussein, but none of these so far have appeared to be quite terrible enough for the highly innovative and dramatic imagination of humanity. However, obligingly, once again we do have a likely name amongst the verses of Nostradamus, that of "Mabus." And nobody has yet deciphered the word, probably because it is much more frightening to imagine that one day there will be a character with that name, or an anagram of it, probably somewhere in the Middle East and probably with two teeth growing out of the back of his throat, or so the legend goes.

Except that there is a far more convincing and exciting explanation if we dig around in the history books.

In the Netherlands town of Breda (then Flemish) in 1478, was born a man named Jan Gossaert, who would become one of the most famous artists of the period, particularly well known for his Italian Renaissance style of painting. Jan's family was French, from the town of Maubeuge, and as artists often did he changed his name for the sake of style. He changed it to Mabuse, Jan Mabuse.

His paintings were among the most famous of his age, that also happened to be Nostradamus' age, almost exactly, for Mabuse lived until 1532, when Nostradamus was 26 years old and very conscious of the Italian Renaissance, along with every other intelligent and cultured individual of the time.

The town from which Mabuse took his name, Maubeuge, means "the bad place." It is the firm belief of the author that Nostradamus used this local and living character's name as an indication of a time and place in our century.

Given this possible new explanation for the word "Mabus," let us look once again at the whole verse:

The two most infamous of the antichrists chosen by interpreters of the prophet's verses are Napoleon and Hitler. Evidence within the verses is convincing though not conclusive in either case and certainly the so-called third antichrist is probably not a single individual at all, but a place.

"The bad place then will soon die, there will come a horrible defeat for people and animals: then suddenly one will see vengeance, hundred, hand, thirst, hunger when the comet will run."

Given that Nostradamus speaks often of the last years of the 20th century as being the worst that mankind has ever experienced in terms of war, destruction, and economic failure, then it makes perfect sense to refer to it as "the bad place." In this way, the Antichrist is no longer a single individual, upon whom we can conveniently heap all our evil, stupidity, and anxiety, as we did with Napoleon and Hitler, but a whole area of life, a place. This place is the world, the deeds, the wars, the horrors, and the pollutions that we have all created.

As we will see in other quatrains, Nostradamus' use of contemporary or historical characters as clues to future events works far more convincingly than complex anagrams or mythological references, particularly so in the case of "Mabus."

In relation to this concept of a "bad place" being our world

eft ~ Los Angeles police break up a party in the ƒreet during riots. Given the constant state of riot ₁nd unrest throughout the world, planet Earth can ₑ seen as a "bad place" during the latter years of ⁣is century.

bove ~ the artist Jan Mabuse took his name from the ₑrench town Maubeuge, meaning "the bad place."

during the end of our century, there is another relevant point. Within the subtleties of astrological prediction, any planetary placement (such as the transit of Pluto through Scorpio or the Uranus/Pluto conjunction of the 1960s that we have discussed) can be applied both to the external physical activities of single individuals and to groups (countries, places). These placements predict war or famine, success, or any other normal human activity. They also predict internal psychological events within individuals or groups of individuals. These involve mass depression and negativity that leads to higher levels of crime, greater instances of divorce and unhappy relationships or positive trends such as religious revivals or economic booms. In other words, the same placements predict both the external and internal changes that concur, and indeed cause one another.

The process appears to depend upon levels of consciousness prevailing at the time of the changes or events. The more unconscious or blind an individual (or country) is, the more predictably extroverted and concrete the planetary expression will be. During the 16th century, for example, there was not a very great sense of "individual" as we now think of it, no real awareness of an "inner" world of the psyche. Consequently, people were much more predictable, hence prophecy was more easily executed through the reading of natal charts, seeing the transits across them at a particular moment in the future. The transits would most likely be expressed through external events only, and not complicated by internal subtleties and alternatives. In short, prophets were more successful in the earlier periods of history than they are today, because consciousness has increased with time.

The most important factor, therefore, in this theory is that our higher consciousness today reflects the planetary placements in many and varied aspects. It is no longer a matter of one dreadful individual causing the deaths of millions of people, but much more that the combined elements within us all affect everything around us: the political, social, ecological, psychological attitudes and events that occur. Put simply, we are our world.

The verse concerning Mabus, then, works to set us on our way through the miasma of the future we are about to face at the end of this millennium and into the 21st century. The most evident aspect of our journey, as illustrated by the quatrains and their astrological support, is that we will become, more than anything else, responsible for ourselves and everything that happens to us in that future.

The Cramped Empire

THE JAPANESE EMPEROR LAYS DOWN HIS SCEPTER

"The great Empire will soon transfer into a small place which will soon come to grow: a very small place in a cramped area, where in the middle he will come to lay down his sceptre."
C1 32

The Japanese Emperor Akihito still has power to lose before the beginning of the next century.

THIS EXTRAORDINARY QUATRAIN gives us almost a blow-by-blow description of Japan. The "great Empire" ruled by a powerful emperor, brought down by World War II, "will soon transfer into a small place...," which then soon came to grow through an extraordinary industrial determination. "...a very small place in a cramped area...."

The Japanese form an unique nation, a single ethnic group that was originally a branch of the Mongolian race. There are now 108 million Japanese people living on an island of 143,818 square miles that constitutes almost 1,000 people for every square mile. The nation grew at a dramatic pace, from 34 million people in 1868, increasing more than three times that in just over a century.

During the 1960s industrial growth was so rapid that this tiny country took the world by storm, increasing by 12% per annum, greater than any other industrialized nation on Earth. During the 80s it was the 3rd largest economic power behind the USA and the former Soviet Union.

We are told of this entire story within these brief four lines, and the last line gives us the future, for it seems that the Emperor will lay down his sceptre in due course.

Under the 1946 constitution, following the war, the new Japanese laws allowed the Emperor to be only a symbol of the state and the unity of the people. Sovereign power now rests in the hands of the people.

Japan renounced war as a sovereign right, and fundamental human rights are now guaranteed as eternal and inviolable.

The Emperor continues to exert only the formalities of his position, such as appointing the Prime Minister and the Chief Justice of the Supreme Court. According to the prediction, even this will be set aside: "...where in the middle he will come to put down his sceptre."

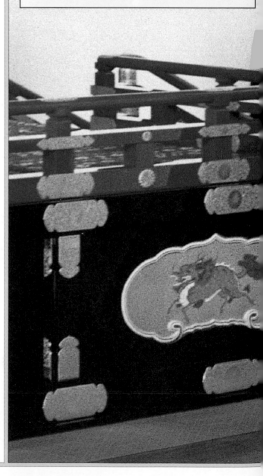

The Fate of Communism & The Baltics

2002 ~ UNITED STATES OF AMERICA & COMMONWEALTH OF INDEPENDENT STATES FALL OUT

La loi Moricque on verra déffaillir:
Aprés une autre beaucoup plus séductive:
Boristhenes premier viendra faillir:
Par dons et langue une plus attractive.
C3 95

"The law of More will be seen to decline: after another much more seductive: Dnieper first will come to give way: through gifts and tongue another more attractive."

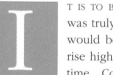

IT IS TO BE EXPECTED that if Nostradamus was truly a successful prophet, then he would be aware of future events that rise high above the average waves of time. Counted among such events would certainly be the extraordinary development of the Soviet Union over the last century and a half. The verse at the top of this page is so clear and precise that we are left breathless with Nostradamus' occasional capability to get his future exactly right. Interpreters such as Edgar Leoni in the 1960s, could not avoid commenting on this as a prediction concerning the fall of communism.

Briefly, the lines indicate that the "law of More" gives us the ideologies of Sir Thomas More's *Utopia* that was the common ancestor of all utopian concepts, bringing life to "Communism," that we are told will be "seen to decline." This will occur after "another much more seductive," being presumably that of democracy from the West. More's work was first published in Latin during Nostradamus' early education so would certainly have been read by him. We are then told that the decline would occur close to the Dnieper, the principle river of the Ukraine. During Nostradamus' lifetime this area was a poor and backward region of Europe, part of the Polish-Lithuanian state for 300 years prior, not one that would have involved much activity during his lifetime. The last line tells us the rest of the story, being involved in "gifts" (economic aid from the rest of the world) and "tongue," being the discussion and talks that helped decide the Soviet leaders to take the massive step that led Gorbachev and Yeltsin to dismantle Communism. A truly startling prediction.

Elsewhere, among his most successful prophecies is yet another that has already come to fruition in the past few years. In the 1980s the idea that the "Cold War" would end, that the former Soviet Union would make peace with the United States, would have seemed absurd, and yet the prophecy was right there staring everyone in the face.

> *"One day the two great masters will become friends. Their great power will be seen to increase. The new land (America) will be at the height of its power. To the man of blood the number will be reported."*

Another quatrain continues the story, moving us into the future:

> *"The two will not remain united long: within thirteen years they face barbarian power. There will be such loss on both sides that one will bless the barque (of St. Peter) and his cape."*

The "two great masters" are Bush and Gorbachev (USA and USSR). Certainly the US was at the height of its power when the Soviet Union began its descent. "To the man of blood the number will be reported." This refers to Gorbachev's kidnapping by the remaining stalwarts of the Kremlin power center. Evidently the Commonwealth of Independent States

Left ~ *Nostradamus uses Sir Thomas More's book "Utopia" as the clue to direct us towards his vision of communism. More was the first to suggest the idea of a socialist state.*
Above ~ *Gorbachev brought down the communist regime and joined hands with the USA, but according to Nostradamus the story is not yet over and by 2002 the two great powers will fall out again.*
In the verses we can discover the whole story of the communist collapse across the world, including China's continued determination to remain stalwart, though this too comes to an end shortly after the new century begins.

83

and the United States fall out after thirteen years. That would put the date at around 2002. The "Barbare Satrape" refers to a bureaucratic group of provincial governors created in the Achaemenian Empire of Darius I (522-486 BC, one of Nostradamus' favorite periods) called "satraps," who were appointed from the royal Persian family for life to collect taxes, act as supreme judicial authority of each area, and generally behave in an autocratic fashion.

At time of writing (early 1993), the Commonwealth of Independent States appears to be struggling with the problems inherited from decades of communist rule, but they have not as yet fallen seriously into a state of war.

The Union of the Soviet Socialist Republics was the largest single country in the world, occupying the whole of the northern part of Asia, an area of over 8,500,000 square miles (22,403,000 square kilometers), occupied by more than 290,000,000 people in 1990. And this was just the Union itself. The communist influence extended far beyond its borders to Poland, Czechoslovakia, Yugoslavia (as it was), Hungary, Romania, and even to some extent into Italy and Finland. The Chinese are still intent on maintaining the communist concept, though this does not last beyond 2001 as we will see from the Chinese natal astrology in the coming pages.

The vast size and power of the old Union might seem too massive an influence to fall apart as it did without some manifest chaos still to come. However, the astrological indications are that the worst has actually passed.

We have seen the terrible results within the countries that once formed Yugoslavia. The breakup between Bosnia and the other countries in this region could well be just the beginning of further upheaval in the post-communist world, but Nostradamus gives us a preventative scenario.

Above ~ *"Check-point Charlie"*
Right ~ *The first crack in the Perestroika. Even to those of us who have lived through the changes during the past years, it seems almost too dramatic to be true. In the mid-1980s, who would have imagined that the Berlin Wall would be brought down and that the communist Soviet Union would fall apart this century, let alone at such speed. Yet four hundred years ago, Nostradamus saw all this happening, and saw also the consequences of these extraordinary events, and how they would affect the rest of the world into the future.*

Libra verra regner les Hesperies,
De ciel et terre tenir la monarchie:
D'Asie forces nul ne verra péries,
Que sept ne tiennent par rang la hiérarchie.
C4 50

"Libra (balance or justice) will see the reign of Hesperias (the West), the sky and Earth held by the monarchy. The forces of Asia will not perish so long as seven maintain the hierarchy in order."

Libra signifies justice and balance, the forces of social order. These will be maintained, it seems, by the Western democratic world. Democracy will prevail ("the sky and Earth held by the monarchy") over communism. The forces of Asia, in this case the old USSR, will not perish as long as the seven countries of the Warsaw pact (this is the only applicable seven nation group that we can choose) remain in a state strong enough to sustain the major changes that will occur. The seven nations are the Baltic States (ex-USSR), what was East Germany (GDR), Poland, Romania, Hungary, Czechoslovakia, and Bulgaria.

Hesperia was the Latin word signifying the land of the West, and derived from the Greek "Hesperus," the evening star, brother of Atlas, and father of the "Daughters of Evening."

Nostradamus is implying in this verse that the fabric of these countries, like a carefully stitched corset around an uncertain frame, must be maintained in order, so that the breaking up of the Communist unions can be without trauma.

Yugoslavia was not part of the Warsaw Pact and may therefore be seen as a separate center of troubles with no potential influence over the other Communist countries.

From the astrological viewpoint, there is an available natal chart for the original Warsaw Pact (that, with its time and place gives us a starting point for the USSR), that contains a sixteen and a half degree Leo ascendant.

Within the pages of this book we will be using a number of natal charts, or birth charts, for different countries. These are exactly the same system as can be applied to single individuals. Put another way, as an individual is born at a certain time of the day or night, so an event, such as the birth of a country, is also "born" at a specific time. This provides us with an astrological starting point for future predictions based on horoscopes which suggest tendencies through the positions of the planets at specific moments in the future. The interpretations provided are in each case backed up by the illustrated presence of the actual natal charts in each case.

According to the natal chart on the following page for the "birth" of the Warsaw Pact, during the late 80s and early 90s Pluto transited in

Nostradamus indicates to us that the Baltic States will not go the way of countries that were part of Yugoslavia.

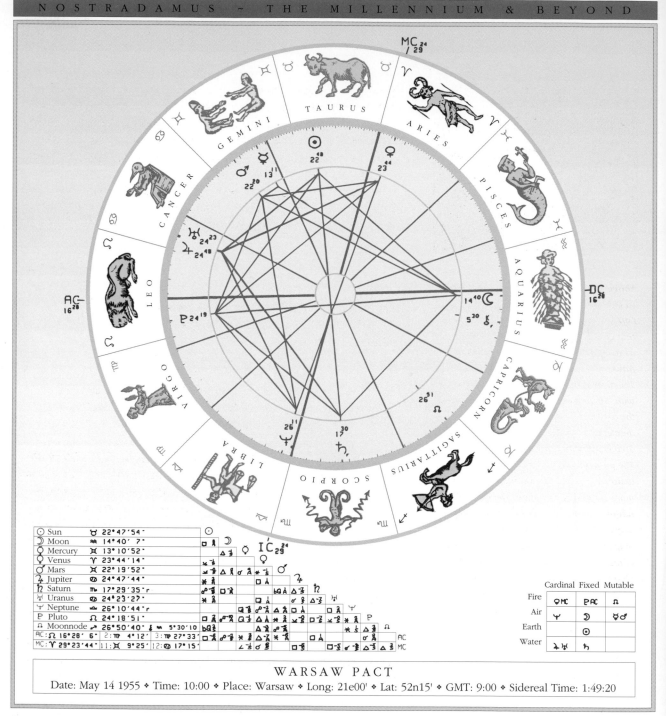

	Sun	☉	22°47'54"
	Moon	♒	14°40' 7"
	Mercury	♓	13°10'52"
	Venus	♈	23°44'14"
	Mars	♓	22°19'52"
	Jupiter	♋	24°47'44"
	Saturn	♏	17°29'35" r
	Uranus	♋	24°23'27"
	Neptune	♎	26°10'44" r
	Pluto	♌	24°18'51"
	Moonnode	♌	26°50'40" ♂ 5°30'10"
	AC: ♌ 16°28' 6"	2: ♍ 4°12'	3: ♍ 27°33"
	MC: ♈ 29°23'44"	11: ♓ 9°25'	12: ♋ 17°15"

	Cardinal	Fixed	Mutable
Fire	♀MC	♇♆	♎
Air	♈	☽	☿♂
Earth		☉	
Water	♃♅		♄

WARSAW PACT
Date: May 14 1955 ✦ Time: 10:00 ✦ Place: Warsaw ✦ Long: 21e00' ✦ Lat: 52n15' ✦ GMT: 9:00 ✦ Sidereal Time: 1:49:20

Above ~ *Military crack-down – problems in Lithuania.*

Left ~ *The first of the national natal charts that give us a clear starting point for our astrological trip from the past through to the future.*

The birth of the Warsaw Pact provides us with the characteristics that we can apply to the old Eastern Bloc countries and their development through the last decade of the 20th century and into the 21st.

The national natal chart is a useful tool to assist us in grounding the predictions with a more scientific foundation. The birth of a nation or agreement operates in the same way as the birth of an individual, for we can map the planets that were around at the time of the birth and apply these to give us the character of the nation and therefore its tendencies in the future.

square (very disruptive) to this ascendant until approximately the end of 1992. In addition there is another natal chart available for Bolshevik Russia that in turn has its Sun in Scorpio, exactly on the Warsaw Pact ascendant, also transited by Pluto in the same three year period.

All this implies great change and massive movement on a national level, the fruition of which we have seen in the collapse of Communism in the region. The worst, astrologically, is over, so that indications are that the "seven" will manage to hold the fabric of the Baltic States together without further major upheaval.

Nouvelle et pluie subite, impétueuse
Empêchera subit deux exercites.
Pierre ciel, feux faire la mer pierreuse,
La mort de sept terre et marin subites.
C2 18

"New and sudden fiery rain will suddenly prevent two exercises (probably military). Stones from the sky, fire makes the sea stony, the death of seven lands and sea suddenly."

This quatrain has been variously interpreted as being the fall of the Eastern Bloc, an unidentified concurrence of natural events, or a battle during the reign of Henry III of France in 1587. The main confusion arises from the fact that in the last line of the French, the word "terre" is in the singular and therefore may not refer to the descriptive "seven." This would mean it was not seven lands and would therefore not apply to the Eastern Bloc countries. It is as though fate hangs in the balance in this case.

In the event that there is a massive and sudden rainstorm that coincides with a falling of stones into the sea, that in turn prevents two military exercises taking place, then this quatrain would anticipate the failure of the seven original Eastern Bloc countries to maintain the awkward balance presently existing in this part of the world. But it wouldn't seem to be a serious threat.

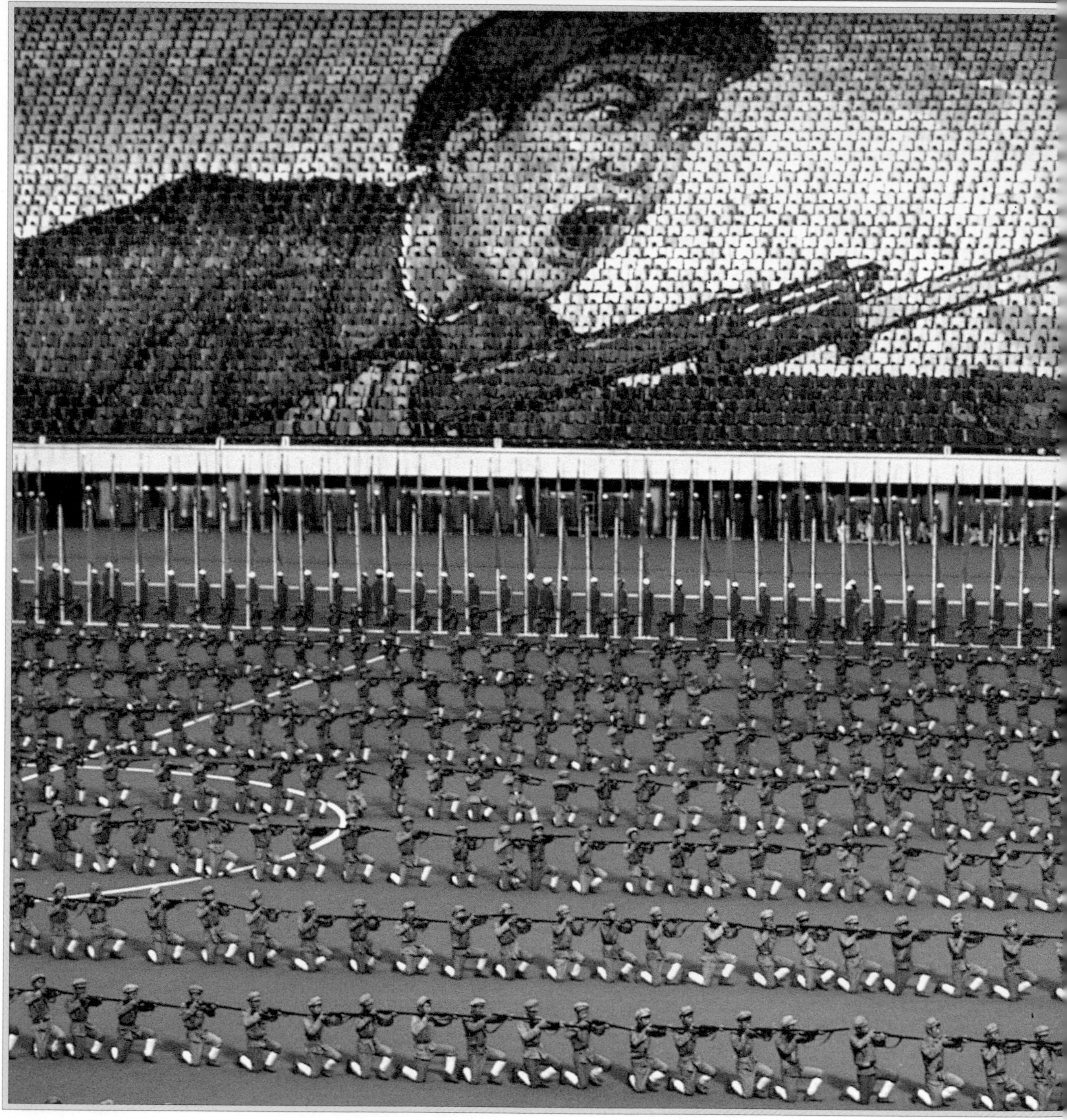

Communist China is the last remaining bastion of an idealistic concept which is dying throughout the world. In Nostradamus' vision, the old rulers of China will soon be gone and at last the young can begin to make their mark **Opposite** ~ In North Korea, a public rally promotes idealistic communism in Kim Il Sung Stadium, Pyongyang.

Natal China

2002 ~ Communism dies in China

THE PROCLAMATION OF the People's Republic of China took place on October 1, 1949 at noon (*The Book of World Horoscopes* – Nicholas Campion). Like East Germany, this natal chart has a Sun/Neptune conjunction in Libra, which reflects the same kind of utopian philosophy. Despite this noble concept the chart also has a Mars/Pluto conjunction in Leo, reflecting great ruthlessness. Between the years 2011 and 2012 Pluto transits to form a square to China's natal Sun when it in turn transits through Capricorn. This suggests a great upheaval in the structure of government. The way the astrological natal chart works, however, is very subtle, because prior to this upheaval we can see the process begin, somehow secretly.

Between 2001 and 2003, Pluto crosses Communist China's ascendant in 16 Sagittarius, thus reflecting a politico-religious idealism, or a kind of fanaticism, similar in character to the religious fanaticism that is currently taking place within fundamentalist Christian America. This transit indicates that Communist China will begin to undergo serious problems at the beginning of the next century, though they will not surface in a major way, evident to the rest of the world, for some ten years more until 2011, when Pluto goes square with the natal Sun. Nostradamus' position in relation to Communist China can be seen in a verse that interpreters have been fascinated by over the centuries.

In Century 4, verse 32, he writes:

> *"In places and times of flesh given fish (or fish-meat), the law of the commune will be made contrary: it will remain strong for the old ones, then removed from the center, the loving of everything in common put far behind."*

Most of Nostradamus' predictions concerned with communism contain some reference to the Ukraine, thus associating them in the interpreter's mind with Communist Russia or the USSR region. In this case there is no such reference, but a rather obscure mention of "flesh" and "fish," which

implies either a Christian location (flesh given fish) or simply an area of the world that thrives on fish. We cannot, through this aspect of the verse, secure the region in China particularly, though given the fact that we are not involved in the Communist Soviet Union or East Germany, China is the other largest area of communist interest. The most significant part of the verse is the line: "...it will remain strong for the old ones, then removed from the center..." The "old ones" refers to the current Chinese political leaders who have remained in power and who still maintain the strict communist rule over their country. By the year 2001 these "old ones" will have been "...removed from the center..." to give way to new rulers who will put far behind "...the loving of everything in common."

Above ~ *the idealism of communism has always given rise to the waving of flags, a concept that has become distrusted this century.*
Right ~ *the entrance to The Forbidden City – Mao's mausoleum. Nostradamus tells us that this last stand will not stand for long and that by the early years of the next century, China will undergo serious upheaval that will result in ultimate downfall of the regime, so that by then the entire world will be free of at least one aspect of human repression.*

The Age of the Iris

2015 ~ A GOLDEN AGE BEGINS

THE FIRST SERIES OF PROPHECIES from Nostradamus' volumes of *The Centuries* is among the most revealing. There is no direct evidence of the way he worked on his quatrains, of whether he strung them together one after another, several in a night, or whether he wrote them over a period and then assembled them into some sort of order according to events supposedly seen in the future. But occasionally we can get a sense of a continuing story running through several quatrains, particularly when applied to the end of this millennium and the beginning of the new one. In *Century* one there appears to be just such a continuity between verses 15 and 17 that follows.

Mars nous menace par sa force bellique,
Septante fois fera le sang épandre:
Auge et ruine de l'Ecclésiastique et plus ceux qui
Deux rien voudront entendre. Faux à létang
Joint vers le Sagittaire en son haut AUGE de
L'exaltation, peste, famine, mort de main militaire:
Le siécle approche de rénovation.
Par quarante ans l'Iris n'apparaitre,
Par quarante ans tous les jours sera vu:
La terre aride en siccité croâtra,
Et grands déluge quand sera apercu.

"Mars threatens us with his warlike strength, seventy times will he caused blood to flow: fall and ruin of the clergy and more for those who will wish to understand nothing from them. The scythe joined to the pond towards Sagittarius at the height of its ascendant, plague, famine, death by military hand: the century approaches its renewal. For 40 years the Iris will not appear, for 40 years it will be seen every day: the arid earth will grow drier and great floods when it will appear."

The iris was a powerful symbol for Nostradamus, and also formed part of his natural remedy portfolio. But was the word iris used to mean rainbow or simply the name of the flower and no more than this?

This trilogy of verses is a truly mammoth prediction. There are a number of clues but first we can try to place the chronology of events. The astrological reference of the pond and scythe at the ascendant of Sagittarius brings us to a very precise date, January 16th, 2015, when this conjunction next takes place. The last such conjunction was in 1985. By this date, according to other quatrains, we will already have seen "the fall and ruin of the clergy," as we will see in Chapter Five of this book. Nostradamus was right about the "plague, famine, death by military hand" – we will be wholly familiar with this story by the beginning of the next century. He tells us that there will have been seventy wars prior to this time, running from the beginning of the 20th century.

But then we move to the last part of the story. It is almost as though this one set of three verses transforms us from present into future; from the wars, plagues, famine, and fallen clergy into a period where the "Iris" speaks louder than suffering. Nostradamus uses the word "Iris" in the original French, and it is up to us to decide what he meant by it. The great majority of interpreters in the past 400 years have taken the word to mean rainbow. The Latin word "Iris" means rainbow, and the Greek goddess Iris was goddess of the rainbow with the responsibility of bringing water from the River Styx when the gods wished to perform some holy ritual. It seems, therefore, a reasonable assumption that this is what he intended, at least if we look no deeper. Interpreters such as Erica Cheetham and Edgar Leoni have, unusually, taken the word rainbow literally, believing that the reference to it signifies rain or the lack of it – that for 40 years there will be no rain and then for another 40 years it will rain every day. But Nostradamus implies that the two phenomena will happen concurrently, not one after the other: "For 40 years the Iris (rainbow) will not appear, for 40 years it will be seen every day: the arid Earth will grow drier and great floods when it will appear."

The Earth will witness both great rain and great drought. In what circumstances could this happen? Perhaps then, this Iris is not a rainbow but simply a flower.

Let's go back a moment and take a look at the prophet once again.

Man of Flowers

D R. DE NOSTRADAME WAS a revolutionary physician. He refused to use the blood-sucking methods of the medical profession on his patients and instead went out into the fields and gathered rose petals (or perhaps many different flower petals), took them back to his makeshift laboratories in the towns where he worked, dried and crushed them into a powder and gave the powder under the tongue of the patient to provide a perfect and very sophisticated natural remedy. In the 20th century this skill is called herbal medicine.

We know only of the story that Nostradamus used the rose petals for the plague, but it is unlikely that the doctor worked with only one flower. He certainly had a wide knowledge of homeopathy, particularly as he also worked as a cosmetician, mixing and providing creams and perfumes to the ladies of the French court.

The iris was no doubt one of his special collection of natural remedies, and if we look at the curative and cosmetic applications of the iris we perhaps begin to make some fresh sense out of this extraordinary prediction.

The iris is of the family *Iridales* and there are some 1,500 species of it around the world. The family Iridales is well known for its medicinal uses, and particularly the iris *Florentina, pallida,* and *germanica*, all of which are found in rich concentration in the areas of southern France where Nostradamus lived and worked. The dried material produced from these flowers is called "orrisroot," and, once the oils are extracted and used for perfumes and soaps, the remaining powders are used for their

The man of flowers formulated more effective cures than were available amongst his garlic-ridden medical colleagues. He used them so effectively to cure the plague that the medical profession shunned him as a revolutionary.

curative properties in relation particularly to helping cure depression.

It would seem much more within the character of this doctor of natural medicine, this poet and prophet, to have used the word iris in a quatrain to mean just that, the iris. And with that in mind perhaps we can take a look at the last part of the quatrains once again.

> *"For 40 years the Iris (rainbow) will*
> *not appear, for forty years it will be*
> *seen every day: the arid Earth will*
> *grow drier and great floods when it*
> *will appear."*

In our chronological event series we have fairly well established that we are talking of the last years of this millennium and the first few of the next, perhaps a span of 40 years? Forty years of general depression, war, famine, plague, when the Iris might well not be seen, metaphorically, at all. And then we enter a further 40 years of the new millennium, the beginning perhaps of the presence of a cure for depression growing right beneath our feet each day. Coincidentally, or perhaps deliberately, the Aquarian Age begins its central cycle around about the year 2050, close to 40 years from the year 2015, the date of the astrological conjunction mentioned in the verse that begins this prediction. This then we can take to be the beginning of the Golden Age, the Age of the Iris.

The Golden Age

2000 ~
1000 YEARS OF PEACE

Above ~ *Apocalypse: the dragon bound and cast into the bottomless pit, a drawing made during the 13th century, inspired by the Apocalypse of St John.*

"...en aprés l'Antéchrist sera le prince infernal, encore par la derniére fois trembleront tous les Royaumes de la Chrétient, et aussi des infideles, par l'espace de vingt cinq ans, et seront plus griéves geurres et batailles, et seront villes, cités, chateaux et tous autres édifices brulés, désolés, détruits, avec grande effusion de sang vetsal, mariées, et veuves violées, enfants de lait contre les murs des villes allidez et brisés, et tant de maux se commettront par le moyen de Satan, prince infernal, que presque le monde universel se trouvera défait et déesolé: et avant ineux avnements aucuns oiseaux insolites crieront par l'air: Hui, hui, et seront aprés quelque temps évanouis. Et aprs que tel temps aura duré longuement, sera preque renouvelé un autre regne de Saturne, et siécle d'or: Dieu le Créateur dira entendant l'affliction de son peuple Satan sera mis et leé en l'abime du barathre dans la profonde fosse: et adonc commencera entre Dieu et les hommes une paix universelle, et demeurera lié environ l'espace de mille ans, et tournera en plus grande force, la puissance Ecclésiastique, et puis tourne délié."

"After that Antichrist will be the infernal prince again, for the last time. All the Kingdoms of Christianity will tremble, even those of the infidels (Islam), for the space of 25 years. Wars and battles will be more grievous and towns, cities, castles, and all other edifices will be burned, desolated, and destroyed, with great effusion of vestal blood, violations of married women and widows, and suckling children dashed and broken against the walls of towns. By means of Satan, Prince Infernal, so many evils will be committed that nearly all the world will find itself undone and desolated. Before these events, some rare birds will cry in the air: Today, today, and some time later will vanish. After this has endured for a long time, there will be almost renewed another reign of Saturn, and a golden age. Hearing the affliction of his people, God the creator will command that Satan be cast into the depths of the bottomless pit, and bound there. Then a universal peace will commence between God and man, and Satan will remain bound for around a thousand years, and then all unbound."

Utopian idealism in the history of mankind has very often led to hell rather than heaven. Hitler's dream was utopian as was the philosophy of communism. It is not necessarily so that this has occurred because of the dream of utopia itself, but because mankind has a habit of fouling up dreams.

Nostradamus does not tell us that we will find utopia, but that shortly after the beginning of the next millennium there will be a long period of peace. War will cease to be of significant interest to humanity for a period of 1000 years. Such a possibility seems almost absurd during the last years of this century, but the predictions are convincing and have been echoed by other prophets also.

IT IS EASY TO IMAGINE, with all this catastrophe and chaos, that mankind is simply on a downward spiral into hell and that nothing can recover our global failure. We have experienced such a long period of history, virtually without let-up, in which war has been the primary occupation of mankind, that we are conditioned to believe there simply cannot be anything else. Most of Nostradamus' interpreters uphold this tradition of his prophecies, that he was a doom-monger and only a doom-monger, and we can see why if we scan the quatrains. But that is only the part that we see, because that is our conditioned nature. There is much more, and for the last part of this chapter on world affairs, we will set about the task of revealing the more positive side of the great doctor and marmalade maker, in relation to events that are due to unfold in the next century.

We hear of this golden age both from Nostradamus' preface to his

Street scenes such as this, from Harlem in New York City, bring a deep sense of insecurity to those who do not have to live in such surroundings. The buildings are empty and covered in graffiti, while the people pass by without even consciously noticing. The Nostradamus doom-interpreters would have us all living this way by 1999, but closer examination of the prophet's verses tells a different story.

son and also within the epistle written to his King, Henry II, excerpted at the beginning of this piece.

> *"For according to the celestial signs, the Golden Age shall return, and after all calculations, with the world near to an all-encompassing revolution... This will be after the visible judgment of heaven, before we reach the millennium which shall complete all."*

Taken from the preface that Nostradamus wrote for his son César, this passage outlines the next step in the grand plan. At the beginning of this chapter we examined how the most precise piece of prophetic dating led to the coming of Jean-Jacques Rousseau into Paris, 177 years, 3 months, and 11 days after the writing – the start of the fall of the Catholic Church, the French Revolution, and the end of the Piscean Age. The next step was to be the "revolution," a kind of continuous holocaust of chaos and destruction. As we have discussed, many interpreters have believed this to mean that we will enter a massive third world war in the last year of the millennium, but, as we have discussed, seen from Nostradamus' perspective it would be quite clear that the whole of the 20th century is a holocaust.

We have had a taste of some of the events still to unfold at the end of this era, particularly in areas that have suffered the Communist regime, as the quote above states: "with the world near to an all-encompassing revolution..." We are presently in that era: "This will be after the visible judgment of heaven, before we reach the millennium which shall complete all."

So, if we believe this remarkable man, the almost "all-encompassing revolution" is due to end, not begin, in the late 1990s. And then we may face the so-called Golden Age, a thousand years of peace.

World Government

Par l'univers sera fait un Monarque,
Qu'en paix et vie ne sera longuement:
Lors se perdra la piscature barque,
Sera régie en plus grand dtriment.
C1 4

"For the world there will be made one monarch, who will not long
be at peace or alive: at the time, the fishing boat (the Papacy) will
be lost, it will also be ruled to great detriment."

 F WE FOLLOW THE CHAIN OF EVENTS throughout the quatrains, we see that Nostradamus was very definite about the end of the Catholic Church (see Chapter 5). He timed its transformation for around the turn of this millennium, and if we value that prediction we may use it as a pointer to the one at the top of this page.

Nostradamus indicates that a single world leader will emerge. For such an event to occur, there would have to be a growth towards a global government. The European Community is the world's first major attempt to unify several established national entities together under one rule. The success of this venture (see Chapter 4) will point the way toward greater unity among the countries of the rest of the world. It seems during the 1990s that there is a willingness to move closer together, and yet many events and attitudes still force us to move further apart. The individual countries fight for their independence, their languages, their economy, yet they find themselves needing one another more and more in order to survive the changes of the new age that is upon us.

At the time of writing there are already many world federations – the World Economics Federation, The World Employment Program, the World Federation for Mental Health, the World Federation of Friends of Museums etc. It seems that many of us already wish to join hands and make this

The United Nations has taken its role as world peace-maker seriously in the years since World War II. The United States also acts as a world police force in many instances of war between other nations. The next step we will see is a worldwide force set up to monitor local problems.

It is believed by many modern thinkers that a global military force is needed to stop war. This force would have to be so powerful that its weaponry would be nuclear. Preventing war by threatening to make war is a bad solution. An anti-nuclear demonstration in London, April, 1987, on the anniversary of the Chernobyl disaster.

into one planet. But the politicians are generally the last to agree.

The source of the need for, and inevitably therefore the antagonism toward, a full-scale world government on Earth comes from the prevalence of war. The original purpose of the United Nations was to end war after the shock and horror of the two so-called "Great" wars. Nobody wanted to fight another war. The UN today still attempts to act as a peacekeeping force in countries such as Bosnia and Croatia during wartime, and in the Gulf War the international laws instituted by the United Nations were kept at the forefront of the war between Iraq and the western allies. The principle is there already.

According to a number of modern thinkers, the only solution to national conflict and individual state anarchy is through the existence of a global military force that is so great and so terrifying that no single nation would dare to break the rules. The basis of this thinking is that if there is no room for war, then people stop thinking about solutions to problems that include war. It seems that the human race is not sufficiently intelligent to maintain a set of personal values that would prevent aggression, so the suppression of those warlike tendencies is the only way. Stop war by the extreme threat of death. This policy has existed in one sense for some time, in fact since the invention and testing of the nuclear bomb and its actual use against the Japanese at Nagasaki and Hiroshima. The existence of the so-called "nuclear deterrent" presumably helps to stop some nations from attacking others.

The negative side of world government, in the minds of many, is that national interests are often fueled and fired by war. War brings a nation together as one, they say. But this false concept is easily debunked, for how much better would it be if the people of the world would come together as one. Nostradamus' verse tells us that the first attempt at world leadership will be short-lived and the first leader (monarch) will not succeed, nor live too long. But we occupy an age of constant experiment, and perhaps in the early part of the 21st century, as indicated by this quatrain, we will see yet another global story begin.

Chapter 3

INSIDE AMERICA

*"The Kings and princes will erect enact
ments, soothsayers make hollow forecasts:
the Corn Mother, golden victim and the
blue skiesbecome acrid. Interpretations
will be rooted out."*

*"They will come to complain about empty
pockets and cry over choices: making mistakes now and again. They will not wish to
remain guided by them, for they will be
deceived by their words."*

N THIS CHAPTER it is the turn of the United States to come
under the hammer of the prophet's poetic verses. And
to make our task easier we have drawn the astrological natal chart of the United States, based on its birth-
date of July 4, 1776 at 5:14 pm local time (given by
Dane Rudhyar in *The Astrology of America's Destiny*, Random House,
1974), the date of the unilateral declaration of independence from
England.

The chart, reproduced on these pages, gives us a broad picture of
the development that the country passes through around the end of this
millennium and into the 21st century.

Used in conjunction with the chosen quatrains we can get a clear
story of the way in which the future will unfold.

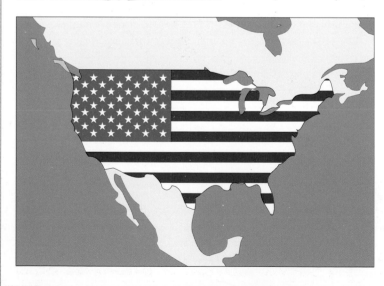

*The natal chart of the birth of the
United States of America, dated at
5.14 p.m. local time on July 4,
1776. From the first natal scream
of America we can move forward
into the evolution of its future.*

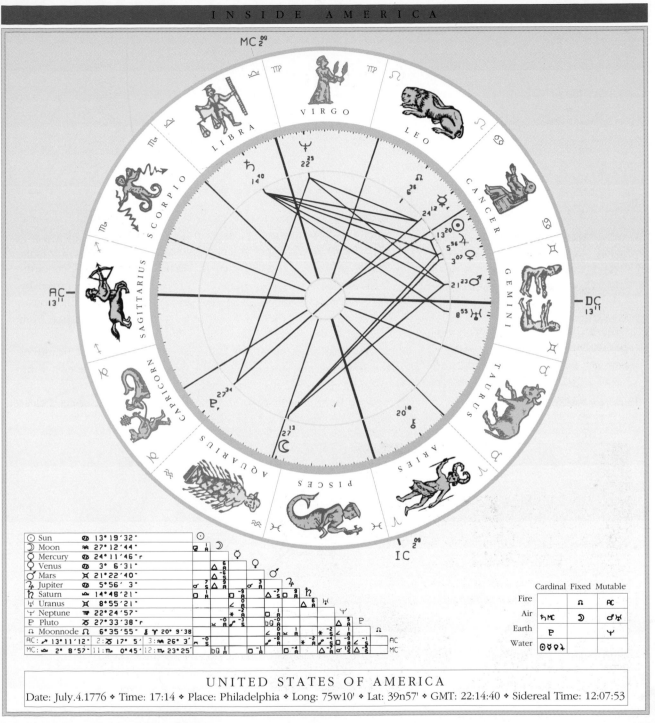

☉ Sun	♋ 13°19'32"		
☽ Moon	♒ 27°12'44"		
☿ Mercury	♋ 24°11'46" r		
♀ Venus	♋ 3° 6'31"		
♂ Mars	♓ 21°22'40"		
♃ Jupiter	♋ 5°56' 3"		
♄ Saturn	♎ 14°48'21"		
♅ Uranus	♓ 8°55'21"		
♆ Neptune	♍ 22°24'57"		
♇ Pluto	♑ 27°33'38" r		
☊ Moonnode	♌ 6°35'55" ☍ ♈ 20° 9'38"		
AC: ♐ 13°11'12"	2: ♑ 17° 5'	3: ♒ 26° 3'	
MC: ♎ 2° 8'57"	11: ♏ 0°45'	12: ♏ 23°25'	

	Cardinal	Fixed	Mutable
Fire		♌	AC
Air	♄ MC	☽	♂ ♅
Earth	♇		♆
Water	☉ ♀ ♃ ☿		

UNITED STATES OF AMERICA

Date: July.4.1776 ✦ Time: 17:14 ✦ Place: Philadelphia ✦ Long: 75w10' ✦ Lat: 39n57' ✦ GMT: 22:14:40 ✦ Sidereal Time: 12:07:53

The Buck Stops

1994 ~ RECESSION LIFTS

THE ECONOMIC RECESSION that descended on the United States in the early years of the 1990s seems likely to lift early in 1994 according to the astrological indications shown on the natal chart. There will be an upturn that will continue for some seven years through to just past the beginning of the 21st century and the turmoil that America has been facing on the economic front will turn into a more political disruption as the first decade runs out.

According to the signs available to us from Nostradamus and the astrological readings, there is no boom time just around the corner, but there is a more settled period that will erupt again into problems later.

In the first quatrain of this chapter we are given a general picture of economy and politics that began to be applicable in the early 1990s. A brief explanation of the lines will help to clarify:

> *"The Kings and princes will erect enactments, soothsayers make*
> *hollow forecasts: the Corn Mother, golden victim and the blue skies*
> *become acrid. Interpretations will be rooted out."*

Nostradamus refers to "Kings and princes" meaning the politicians and rulers. He tells us that they will be making "hollow forecasts." This is not news. Politicians have been forced into making promises and determinations that almost invariably turn out to be false simply because it is now impossible to predict the way the political and economic climate is changing during this era. We cannot really blame the politicians because we have created a system that is rapidly becoming unworkable.

Nostradamus next refers to "the Corn Mother, golden victim and the blue skies become acrid." The Corn Mother is a mythological figure, who has been around since the beginning of time and has appeared in most of the major cultures such as the Middle East, Crete, Greece, Egypt, and Rome. She gave birth to the maize that is the foundation of the human staple diet and is Demeter or Gaia, the Earth itself. Her story is one of

According to Nostradamus the Aquarian Age will bring a new awareness of the devastating consequences of man's greed and disregard for his environment.

fecundity and good harvest, and Nostradamus uses her here as a metaphor for the current state of the world's ecology, with a particularly apt reference to the "blue skies become acrid," that we might see as the image of light in the skies as a result of the holes in the ozone layer. In effect he is saying that the whole process of social and ecological awareness will alter – the golden harvest, the blue skies – for humanity in the Aquarian Age. The last part of the verse, "Interpretations will be rooted out," refers to the fact that sooner or later we will effect changes and improvements in the shared resources (Aquarius) of our economic and political systems. Efforts will be made toward a more efficient global control over currency and national spending, so that resources can flow better between richer and poorer countries. Aquarius is a Saturn-ruled sign and thus conservationist at heart, but with an orientation towards a more ethical distribution of wealth. The whole idealism of communism went into decline because people, by nature, wish to own a little something that is theirs alone.

The second quatrain reinforces the story:

"They will come to complain about empty pockets and cry over choices: making mistakes now and again. They will not wish to remain guided by them, for they will be deceived by their words."

The problems of recession, poor quality housing, overpopulation, and unemployment, all add to a sense of unfairness among a larger and larger sector of the US population. People will eventually not wish to be guided by the uncertain words of their leaders because all that results is empty pockets. The corn, the golden promises, and the blue skies must change their colors.

The United States of America is the perfect candidate for the biggest and most dramatic outburst of poisons, partly because of its immense power position in the world picture, but also because of a special aspect that relates specifically to secrecy: to the attempts always to cover up the truth. This particular poison must rise to the surface sooner or later according to the prophet and the planets. But before entering into this complex region of America, perhaps we can look at a more obvious symptom of the progress towards the future.

Harsh weather and hard times have afflicted
American farmers, as their government has
persued agricultural policies that favor large
corporations over the smaller family farm.
Nostradamus seems to suggest a shift away
from this shortsighted policy in the future.

Social Disease

THE LATE 1990s ~ AIDS, FULL REALIZATION

O NE OF THE MOST PROFOUND ways in which mankind has expressed his inner poisons over the years around the end of this century is through human diseases.

In his epistle to Henry II, Nostradamus had the following to say about the last years of Pluto's transition:

"The leaders of the Church will be backward in their love for God... Of the three sects the Catholic is thrown into decadence by the partisan differences of its worshippers. The Protestant will be entirely undone in all Europe and part of Africa by the Islamics, by means of poor in spirit who, led by madmen (terrorists perhaps), shall through worldly luxury commit adultery...in the meantime so vast a plague that two-thirds of the world will fail and decay. So many that no one will know the true owners of fields and houses. The weeds in the city streets will rise higher than the knees, and there shall be a total desolation of the Clergy."

The rising panic surrounding the spread of AIDS is more than familiar to us all. If the published statistics are anything to go by, more than a million people in America alone are already visibly infected with the virus. If there is no cure, or at least a profound change in public attitudes and behavior, the figures could be well into the tens of millions by the end of this millennium, along with vast portions of the population in some African and Asian countries. Given his tendency to exaggerate, Nostradamus' prediction that two thirds of the human race would be killed by a plague could be not so far from the truth. But perhaps the predicted plague is not simply that of AIDS, but something far more widespread and more deeply rooted.

It should be remembered that the time of Nostradamus was a time of plague also. The bubonic plague swept through Europe from China during the 15th and 16th centuries in such a way that people believed the whole world would be dead within a few years. The bubonic and pneumonic plagues are still around in the 20th century. In fact, reports in 1992 from California showed that the squirrels and rats in the forests

Disease has always been treated as an isolated concept, and as each new form of disease arises, so we scrabble for a cure. But the real disease lies hidden much deeper in society and Nostradamus indicates to us the presence of a complex Multi-Plague that exists at the very roots of society. According to his prophecies there are far larger numbers of "hidden" HIV sufferers than are currently projected during the mid-1990s, which will become evident towards the end of the decade.

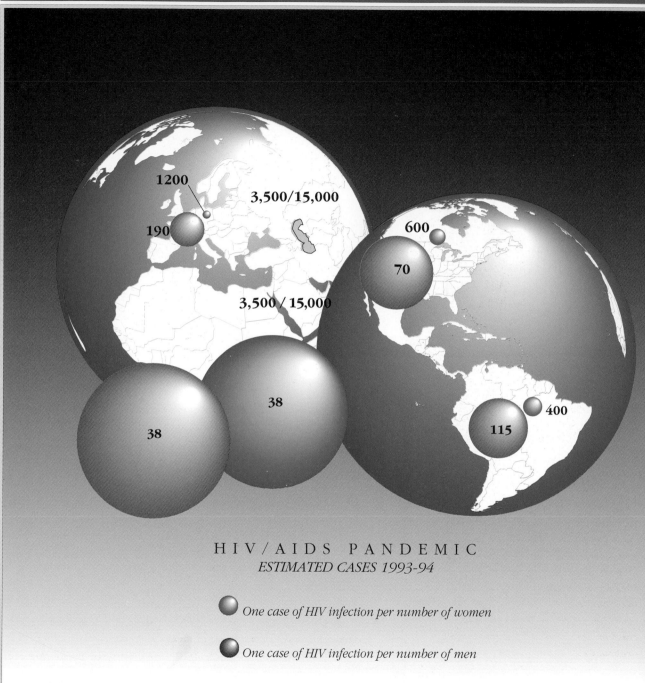

1200

190

3,500/15,000

600

70

3,500 / 15,000

38

38

400

115

HIV/AIDS PANDEMIC
ESTIMATED CASES 1993-94

One case of HIV infection per number of women

One case of HIV infection per number of men

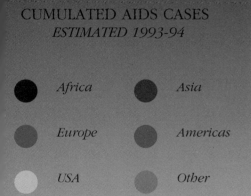

CUMULATED AIDS CASES
ESTIMATED 1993-94

● Africa   ● Asia

● Europe   ● Americas

● USA   ● Other

The World Health Organization's current projection for the year 2000, is that there will be a cumulative total of over 40 million HIV infections in men, woman and children, of which more than 90% will be in the developing countries. There will be over 10 million children less than 10 years of age orphaned as a result of AIDS.

around San Francisco and Los Angeles were carrying the plague in large numbers. During that year, one woman, a school teacher, died of the plague. It took less than one day from the showing of the symptoms to her death. AIDS is not like that. Its growth is much more a mirror of our age. It is enigmatic, changing in shape, and sexually related. The moment one strain of it has been discovered, the structure of the disease appears to change into a different form and attack again. It is as though we have spawned a disease to beat all diseases, except that this sickness is still more complex even than this, for it is not made up of one labeled disease called AIDS but several, like a lethal cocktail.

Above ~ Prejudice and fear neither help the victims of this deadly disease, nor contribute to finding a cure. Unless we make a concerted effort to confront and deal with the tragedy of AIDS, we could see many more scenes like this.

115

The Multi-Plague

Auprés des portes et dedans deux citez
Seront deux fléaux onc n'aperceu un tel,
Faim, dedans peste, de fer hors gens boutez,
Crier secours au Grand Dieu immortal.
C2 6

"On the doorstep of and inside two cities, there will be two pesti-
lences like none ever seen. Hunger, inside pestilence, except for iron,
they will be at the end, crying for help to the great immortal God."

HERE ARE MANY VERSES AMONGST *The Centuries* that predict the coming of a great plague. Each age looks on these predictions as representing a particular disease that will ultimately wipe out mankind or at least the greater part of the race of humanity. In Nostradamus' age the great plague was bubonic. After the World Wars, the great plague was cancer. In our age, at the end of the 20th century, the plague to beat all plagues is AIDS. But this all seems very subjective. We are not seeing our world through the eyes of the Prophet himself, but through our own fearfulness.

It is true that AIDS is a terrible killer and may already have infected a far larger area of population than we realize. But it seems more likely that Nostradamus was seeing something far wider in its influence, something that has a stronger rooting in the very foundations of society and particularly now in the United States.

We could call this plague something completely new. We could call it the "Multi-Plague" because it appears to be made up of several different parts. The basic components of this social epidemic are:

1) The HIV virus; 2) Syphillis; 3) Poverty; 4) Depression; 5) Drug abuse; 6) Ignorance and prejudice.

It is not that these different conditions are independent of one

Nostradamus indicates that the plague of the future will grow inside cities, and therefore, presumably, as a result of city life. The Multi-Plague concept is like a dreadful melting pot of many different ingredients such as depression, syphillis, poverty, drug abuse - all adding up to a social disorder which cannot be cured by medicine alone. Here, a well-dressed drunk provides a striking counter-point to the affluence of a manicured American city.

another, because in recent surveys done within US hospitals and universities laboratories it appears that they all feed off one another. The existence of extreme poverty causes despondency that leads to clinical depression. Poor diet exacerbates this condition. Poor diet is made worse, in turn, by media advertising, for it is the poor quality foods that are more vociferously advertised, particularly on television, the 20th century's ultimate escape mechanism. Depression through poverty and poor diet leads to smoking, alcoholism, and drug abuse. The excessive abuse of drugs then leads to further poverty, and either through a contaminated needle or unprotected sexual relations, the HIV virus is contracted, very often along with syphillis. Syphillis is more rampant in the United States during the 1990s than it has been since the 18th and 19th centuries in Europe. To finally cap the problem, particularly in relation to attitudes toward the gay communities, there is ignorance and prejudice that in the United States has led to a reluctance on the part of the government to put sufficient funds into research for cures. In a hospital in the South Bronx in New York City in 1992, 38% of adults tested were HIV-positive. More than 250,000 cases of the AIDS virus were confirmed during 1992 in New York City alone, making that city a threat to the world, as it contains a highly mobile population.

In effect, the HIV virus, syphillis, drugs, and social deprivations are feeding off one another and building an epidemic that could become the killer that Nostradamus foresaw. And the root of this epidemic is not only medical but also social, economic, political, also emotional and psychological.

It is true that the advent of AIDS in the United States is seen as having derived through the gay community, who are not generally a poor community. The progress of AIDS since inception has developed into poverty stricken areas, and essentially the cure will not be only a medical cure, for this is simply like shifting around the deck chairs on the *Titanic*. The moment we find a vaccine for AIDS, another combination of the multi-plague will pop up right behind it, with similar prejudices and near-sightedness. The cure lies in a change of the whole structure of life, and America is the guinea pig.

"Hunger, inside pestilence, except for iron they will be at the end.."

It is interesting that Nostradamus refers to "inside pestilence," as though somehow the pestilence he is referring to comes from something deep inside us. The reference to "except for iron" refers to the prevalence of continued war and conflict. During our plagues and pestilence we will continue to fight, as always.

One of the main breeding grounds of the Multi-Plague in world society is the poverty and isolation of our big cities. According to the prophet, the cure for the disease of social inequality and the resulting separation from one another is ultimately an understanding of love. In the future, society will be based on the desire inherent in all humans for community mutual support.

Below *~ a group of musicians take their talents to the streets.*

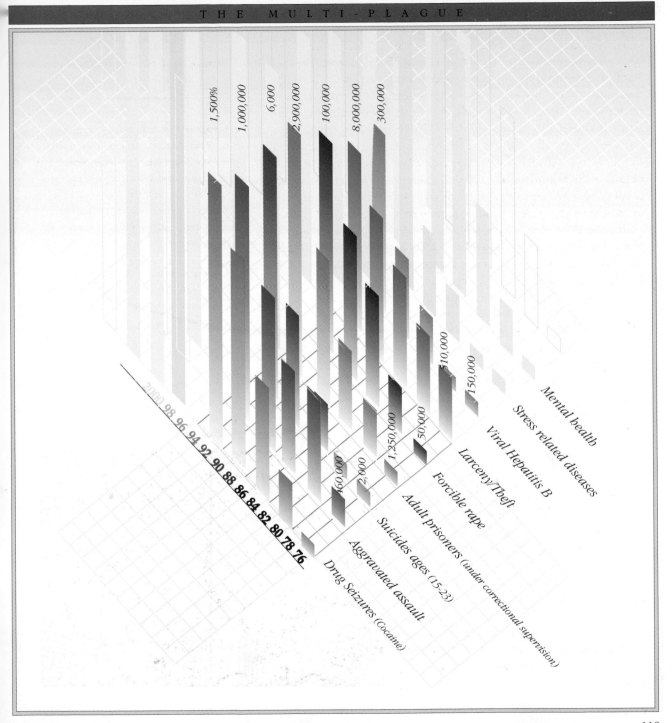

Plan for America

1996-2016 Calm USA

IGHT NOW, DURING THE LAST YEARS of 20th century, it is hard to get a clear view. Especially in the United States, it seems that everything is going wrong and there are no ready solutions. New presidents come and go. The electors still make an enormous fuss, shout and scream with joy, as their new man is elected to power, and within a shorter and shorter time span it becomes clear that they have made yet another mistake. And yet it continues to happen again and again. The people "in power" have no motivation to pull the carpet away from under their own feet. Naturally so. But so long as the carpet fails to fly, so the problems will be there.

However, if we look at the astrological readings, and some other of Nostradamus' quatrains, we can make out a fairly accurate chronological plan of the progress of the United States of America through to the year 2016.

Examining the characteristics created by the planetary positions at the time of America's birth, we find a picture in which we can believe with some degree of confidence. Perhaps one of the most significant aspects within the birth chart of the USA with which we can make some judgment about the future is the Mercury and Pluto opposition. This configuration within an individual's chart signifies a most interesting potential character. Seen as a characteristic of the nation, it would illustrate well, on the positive side, great subtlety, an interest in the invisible or hidden side of life – such as concern in America for psychoanalysis, spiritualism, and religious cults. America was the first country to conduct reputable experiments into parapsychology. This goes along with an ability to penetrate to the truth and recognize the lies of others.

On the negative side, it can reflect obsessive secrecy, deceptiveness, and undercover dealings. It is one of the astrological placements that can (not necessarily will) produce a superb liar.

As a national characteristic, it has its good points, one of which is a willingness to explore the world of the psyche. Other countries, such as

US elections are always the same – a grand drama on the public stage of political enthusiasm. But by the end of the presidency, it often seems like all that was just hot air and the poor guy at the top comes tumbling down.
Above *~ President Clinton at the 1992 Democratic Convention in New York City.*

the United Kingdom and France, seem reluctant to do this. In the UK, even C.G.Jung is not taught within university curriculums, except within the religious departments. In America it is possible to acquire a degree in mythology and there are even discussions on the "West Coast" of starting astrology courses within universities because interest in these hidden aspects of life is not considered "weird."

An area of the negative aspect of the Mercury/Pluto opposition is corruption in economic dealings in the form of secrecy. The amassing of wealth appears as an immoral or unethical activity. Ironically, Americans see themselves as open, honest, and frank in all areas of life. They criticize the British for being withdrawn, lacking in expression of their emotions, and non-communicative. Yet beneath the surface of apparent extroversion, Americans can sometimes be very private about their inner lives. This is supported as a general characteristic by a Mercury/Pluto opposition from Cancer to Capricorn in the American natal chart, which is a specific configuration that reflects a collective difficulty in expressing thoughts and feelings, and communication which appears to be open but which conceals a great deal. The ubiquitous use of jargon, "buzz" and slang words, and "politically correct" expressions all reflect this kind of evasion. This is a general trend rather than a personal failing and suggests that things are never quite what they might appear to be, especially in the way that the country as a whole expresses itself to other countries, and in the way that the government presents itself to the people. This enigmatic characteristic is typical in individuals of the Mercury/Pluto aspect.

We saw this aspect most readily within the 1992 presidential election in which everyone seemed on the surface to be so enthusiastic, flag-waving and excited. But at the same time there were rumors of numerous "dirty-tricks" to discredit the candidates.

This can be seen as a style of communication within the natal chart, even a congenital condition, of putting things always obliquely. This is part of the American way.

The contrasts of American life are self-evident. Where individual enterprise and the glorious dollar are like gods to the people, glamor and glitz will always be contrasted with poverty and crime. This will not change in the future.

Above ~ 1990 riots in Miami after police are acquitted of brutality charges.

So, looking forward through the eyes of astrology, according to the American natal chart illustrated on these pages we find some fascinating changes.

1994 – 1997. The "heavy" planets Uranus and Neptune, transiting together through Capricorn, are approaching a conjunction with America's natal Pluto and an opposition to America's natal Mercury. These aspects peak between February 1994 and December 1997. These suggest a period of sudden major revelations and discoveries, on the positive side, within medicine and technology. On the negative side they suggest instances of scandal in terms of the revealing of dark secrets.

The same aspects would also suggest a period of great confusion, a kind of "losing one's way," both in terms of how the government is run and how the country sees its own role in the world. According to the Dane Rudhyar birth chart of America, the Mercury/Pluto opposition falls into the 2nd/8th house axis, that does in fact deal with finances and shared resources. This indicates a big exposure of a financial scandal during that period, perhaps involving the funding of political campaigns, or the collapse of a large financial monopoly.

The economic situation may be relieved somewhat by some favorable aspects from transiting Saturn at the beginning of Pisces in trine to America's Sun, occurring during 1994. These would stabilize the economic situation sufficiently to deal with, or at least alleviate, the buffeting that is to come.

1996 – 2012. It seems that America will be in for a relatively calm period for 15 years from 1998, and there are a number of interesting transits relevant to this period.

Uranus enters Aquarius in January 1996, and although Neptune is still transiting around the natal aspect of Mercury/Pluto, causing continued confusion and instability, Uranus starts to make more positive aspects. Generally the trend lifts somewhat from 1996, though there are still some negative aspects such as Saturn triggering America's natal Mars in Gemini, square natal Neptune in Virgo, suggesting further feelings of impotence, powerlessness, and confusion.

Eventually, Uranus reaches the conjunction with America's natal Moon in Aquarius, and this heralds a greater role for women in the national psyche. According to this indication we can expect to see a woman president or presidential candidate during the elections of 2004.

Transiting Uranus forms this conjunction throughout 2002 and the first half of 2003. It is not a "global" or malevolent aspect but reflects a period

of great change in terms of the role of women.

There is another less attractive scenario that results from these same transits, and that is the rise of fundamentalist religion, that would in turn reflect a kind of collective emotional "breakdown" state.

2014 – 2016. The astrological readings for this period correspond with the verses that we examined in the previous chapter on global issues.

> *"Mars threatens is with his warlike strength, 70 times will he cause blood to flow: fall and ruin of the clergy and more for those who will wish to understand nothing from them. The scythe joined to the pond towards Sagittarius at the height of its ascendant, plague, famine, death by military hand: the century approaches its renewal. For 40 years the Iris will not appear, for 40 years it will be seen every day: the arid earth will grow drier and great floods when it will appear."*

If we remember, we applied this to the precise date of January 16, 2015, using the reference to the pond and the scythe at the ascendant of Sagittarius.

Once again, according to the natal time in our birth chart for America the ascendant is Sagittarius, which means Saturn will cross the country's ascendant during this period, a time therefore of great soul searching and having to come face-to-face with hard reality. In an individual, such a transit involves a redefinition of a whole life pattern, weeding out the unnecessary and consolidating what is solid. It is not necessarily a terrible configuration, but a sobering one.

America has a tendency also to extremes in religion. The astrological transits of Uranus between 1996-2012 indicate a tendency towards religious fundamentalism. Individual religiousness arises out of freedom, which in turn arises out of intelligent lack of fear. Where fear reigns then freedom dies and everybody rushes for the

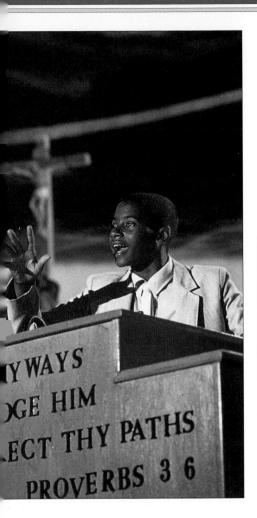

church doors, for death is on the horizon. This tendency began in the early 1990s when fundamentalist groups, created by an increasing fear of the future, grew to prominence. There is a kind of running for cover which permits such organizations to grow and flourish. The ultimate result will always be suffering for effectively freedom is banished by belief.

Saturn will also transit in opposition to America's natal Uranus in Gemini; that suggests a reevaluation of all that was hitherto considered "free" in America.

Another important transit during this same period is that which occurs as Pluto enters Capricorn, bringing it into opposition with America's Venus, Jupiter, and Sun, all lined up in Cancer. In the birth chart, this group of planets is in the seventh house; nationally speaking, the house of allies and open enemies. This transit reflects a complete shift in America's relationship with other countries, economically and through involvements such as NATO. It reflects a conflict and competition on the economic and political level.

Most importantly it reflects a profound change in the nature or definition of government. The transit of Pluto to natal Sun was the aspect in force during the collapse of the Soviet Union, so that we can see the potential scale of this situation in relation to America during this early period of the 21st century.

At the same time, Uranus in Aries is in square to America's Sun in Cancer, so it is certainly a radical transformation. These aspects involve relations with other countries.

Given both Nostradamus' clues and the astrological indications, the next three decades are going to involve some exciting and dramatic changes within the American nation, though certainly there is no indication whatever of the massive holocaust proposed by many of the past interpreters of the quatrains. We are coming now to the end of a holocaust that has been going on for many years.

Chapter 4

THE EUROPEANS

The twelve stars of the European Community flag represent the founder nations.
Although the community is smaller than the rest of the New Europe it boasts over two thirds of the total population.
Europe has a land mass only one quarter that of North America and yet it has a population twice as great. With a population density ranking the third highest in the world it is understandable that in such an overcrowded environment there are intense regional, ethnic and social clashes.
These upheavals have to be faced before there can be any sense of economic or cultural union.

INTERPRETATIONS OF NOSTRADAMUS have been concerned mostly to portray war. Particularly some of the more famous ones see the world as deteriorating into a vast World War Three scenario with Earth ending up looking like something out of Nagasaki. It is as though the interpreters, who perhaps have grown up in a warring environment, can see only war and therefore bring this projection to the table when researching and interpreting the great prophet.

But if we look a bit closer at the verses we see that, although there may still be turmoil within political areas, there is also another flow of ideas that perhaps fits the picture better. And this can be found throughout the verses, in every aspect of life, including those verses that tell us about Europe. The same story that we met in the chapter concerned with the global picture, that begins in the late 1990s with upheaval and difficulties, also applies in the European countries. There are, of course, many quatrains in relation to Europe, but space does not allow us to look at more than a few in this book. We begin therefore with the center of the strife that passes through the new Europe with Pluto's passing through Scorpio and Sagittarius, the holy country of Italy, so holy and yet so corrupt.

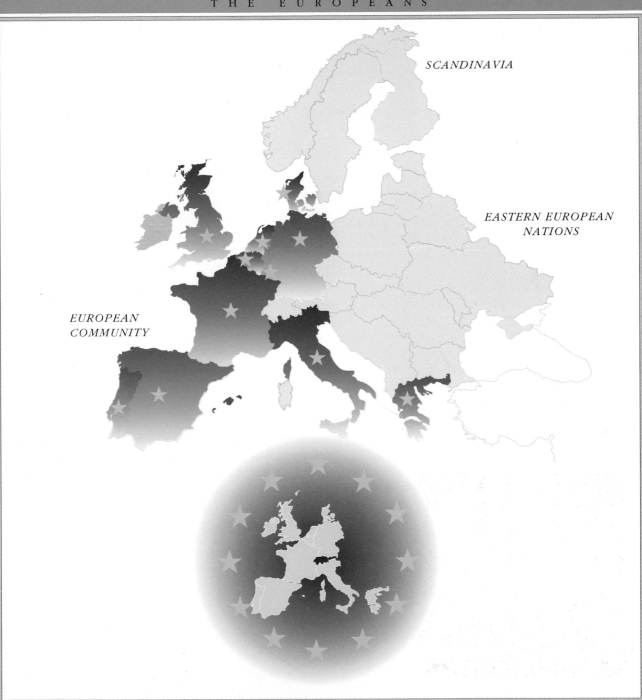

SCANDINAVIA

EASTERN EUROPEAN
NATIONS

EUROPEAN
COMMUNITY

The Italian Revolution

1994 - REVOLT AGAINST THE MAFIA

Au lieu que Hieron fait sa nef fabriquer,
Si grand déluge sera et si subite,
Qu'on n'aura lieu ne terres s'ataquer,
L'onde monter Fesulan Olympique.
C8 16

"In the place where Hieron built his nave, so great and sudden a flood that no place will escape the attack, the wave rising to the Olympic Fiesole."

INTERPRETERS HAVE FOUND the word "Hieron" a major problem. Some have imagined it to be the Greek word meaning holy or divine, and by connecting it with the word "nave" take it to mean Christ's "rock," the Church of Rome. Others have gone so far as to switch it with the word "Jason" to connect it with the reference to Olympic at the end of the quatrain. Some admit that they simply don't know what it means at all.

All this seems very complicated when as usual the answer is simple. If we look at Italian history we find that there was a leader named Heiron who conquered Sicily, coincidentally at the time of the Etruscans. Coincidentally because Fiesole, mentioned in line four, was one of the chief cities of the Etruscan confederacy. Heiron I built religious monuments on Sicily during his rule of the island, and Nostradamus would have been aware of this, as he spent time in Italy and studied its history.

The word "deluge" means flood, and the word "onde" means wave, implying that this is a flood of water. But water could not flood from Sicily to Florence, so we may assume that he was indicating an upheaval such as a revolution or some internal conflict.

At time of writing Sicily is in turmoil because of conflicts between the

people, the local authorities, the Mafia, and the mainland government. The Italian administration is in worse condition than it has been since World War II with stories of corruption and connections with the Mafia itself as though the central government is infiltrated with criminal activities.

This quatrain gives us a firm indication that Italy is in for an internal conflict of major importance after the Olympic games and before the end of this millennium.

There are several quatrains that provide stories of conflict within Italy, both through the downfall or transformation of the Vatican, and through political problems with the Middle Eastern countries. As if revolution were not enough, there is apparently more trouble to come in the south of the boot of Europe from a submarine in 1994.

There have been so many disgusting murders perpetrated by the Mafia in Italy that finally the people will begin a determined revolt against this ancient "family." Nostradamus links together some fascinating themes to indicate to us that the troubles will start in Sicily and move right up the "boot" to Fiesole, near Florence.

Qu'en dans poisson, fer et lettres enfermée,
Hors sortira qui puis fera la guerre:
Aura par mer sa classe bien prame,
Apparoissant pres de Latine terre.
C2 5

"Iron (probably weapons) and letters are enclosed in a fish (submarine), out of which will come one that will make war: his fleet will travel hard across the sea appearing near the Latin land."

If the "crawling" of Pluto through Scorpio and Sagittarius is the detoxification of human affairs, then it seems Italy must contain much poison – for conflicts that will erupt between the Middle East and Europe will inevitably touch Italy directly. This fairly explicit verse has a secondary meaning that has been interpreted as, "When Mars (iron) and Mercury (letters) are in conjunction in Pisces (fish)...." This conjunction dates the prediction in 1994, as this is the next time Mars and Mercury come into conjunction with Pisces.

And Italy's problems may not end there.

Pour la chaleur solaire sus la mer
De Negrepont les poisons demi cuits:
Les habitans les viendront entamer,
Quand Rhod et Gannes leur faudra le biscuit.
C2 3

"By the heat of the sun on the sea at Negrepont, the fish half cooked, the inhabitants will eat them when Rhodes and Gannes will have the biscuit."

This bizarre quatrain refers either to an explosion of nuclear proportions or the burning of the Sun because of a hole in the ozone. The nuclear explosion theory is the most popular. "Negrepont" indicates the island of Ruboea. The quatrain therefore tells us that Italy and Greece are suffering from a lack of food during the time that this great burning takes place in that region. The verse tells us that a major nuclear attack is made in the Mediterranean, though no date is implied.

But the story may not be so bad perhaps, as the astrological readings are not extreme.

Italy's Natal Chart

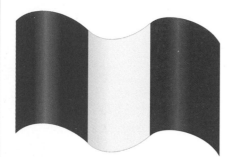

The nation of Italy was effectively born just after World War II, though, of course, the parts that made up the country were born many centuries earlier. Italy's natal chart shows the reasons why such an order as that imposed by the Mafia should be possible, grown out of a tradition of family security which is older than the country itself.

The Mafia system of hierarchical violence was probably born in the Middle Ages to guard against the many conquerors that invaded Sicily, though the term mafia comes from the Italian word "mafie" which was a name given to small armies hired by landowners to protect their properties against bandits.

Nostradamus indicates to us that this terrifying group will lose much of its power before the end of the millennium

T HE CHART USED FOR OUR PURPOSES in looking at Italy's natal position dates from June 10, 1946, and reflects the establishment of a democratic government after World War II. This marked the end of the Italian kingship and Mussolini's rule. Since Italy is still a democracy, it seems an appropriate chart.

According to the astrological interpretation of this chart, there is no major revolution afoot in Italy in the near future, since Italy's Sun in Gemini is not yet being affected by any heavy transits.

However, there is a Venus/Saturn conjunction in the birth chart, in Cancer, that falls in square to the natal Moon. This configuration is a subtle one that operates on an emotional level, bringing a deep conflict between the need for good relations with the outside world (Moon) and a clannish, slightly paranoid, secretive quality that reflects the typically subjective Mafia style of rule, i.e. everyone outside the family is under suspicion.

The natal configuration of Venus/Saturn was triggered by the transiting Uranus and Neptune that started in February 1993 and continues through half of 1994. This supports the presence of upheavals that our interpretation of Nostradamus' quatrains show for Italy. Since it is the Venus/Saturn conjunction that takes the main brunt of the transit, it reflects a real change and lessening of Mafia control.

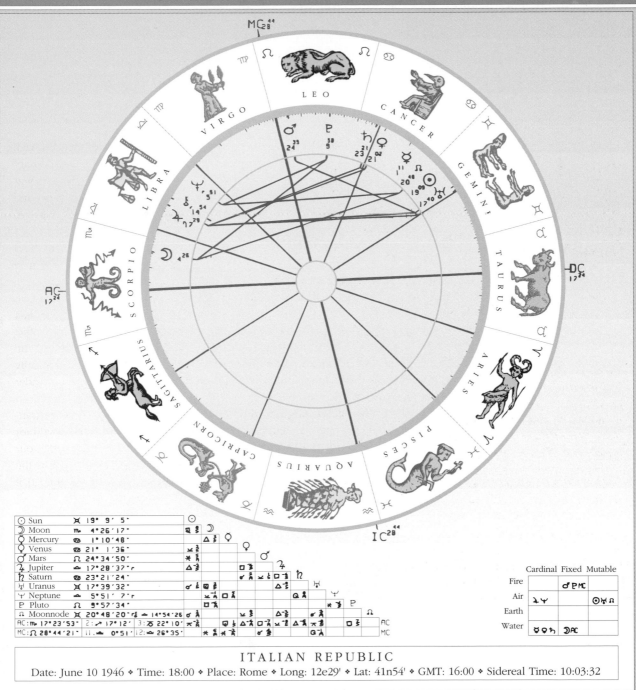

☉ Sun	♓ 19° 9' 5"		☉												
☽ Moon	♏ 4°26'17"	□ ♁ ♃	△ ☽												
☿ Mercury	♋ 1°10'48"			♀											
♀ Venus	♋ 21° 1'36"	⚹ ♃		♂											
♂ Mars	♌ 24°34'50"	△ ♃	⚹ ♄		♃										
♃ Jupiter	♎ 17°28'37" r		⚹ ♄ ⚹ ♃ △ ♄		♄										
♄ Saturn	♋ 23°21'24"	♂ ♀ □ ♃	⚹ ♄ ♄	♅											
♅ Uranus	♊ 17°39'32"		△ ♃		♅										
♆ Neptune	♎ 5°51' 7" r	⚹ ♃ □ ♀	Q ♃	♆											
♇ Pluto	♌ 9°57'34"	□ ♃	⚹ ♃ ♃	P											
☊ Moonnode	♓ 20°48'20" r ☋ ♎ 14°54'26"	♂ ♃	⚹ ♃ △ ♃ ⚹ ♃	☊											
AC: ♏ 17°23'53"	2: ♐ 17°12'	3: ♑ 22°10'	⚹ ♃	□ ♃ △ ♃ □ ♃ ⚹ ♃ △ ♃ ⚹ ♃	□ ♃	AC									
MC: ♌ 28°44'21"	11: ♎ 0°51'	12: ♎ 26°35'	⚹ ♃ ⚹ ♃ △ ♃	♂ ♃	Q ♃	MC									

	Cardinal	Fixed	Mutable
Fire		♂ ♇ MC	
Air	♃ ♀		☉ ♅ ☊
Earth			
Water	♀ ♀ ♄	☽ AC	

ITALIAN REPUBLIC

Date: June 10 1946 ❖ Time: 18:00 ❖ Place: Rome ❖ Long: 12e29' ❖ Lat: 41n54' ❖ GMT: 16:00 ❖ Sidereal Time: 10:03:32

The Italian Peace

A Logmyon sera laissé le regne,
Du grand Selin qui plus fera de faict:
Par les Italies estendra son enseigne,
Regi sera par prudent contrefaict.
C6 42

"To Logmyon (Ogmius) will be rejected the kingdom of Selin (the Moon) who will do more. He will extend his sign to Italy, and will counteract through prudence."

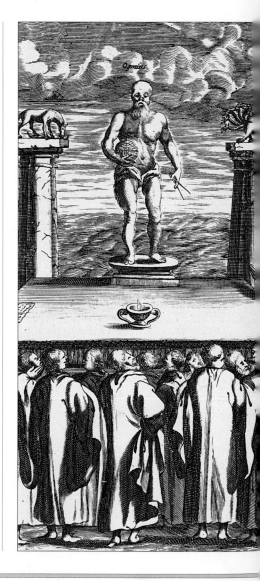

F WE INTERPRET THE STRANGE WORD "Logmyon" as Ogmius, we find a first hint to help us on our way through this enigmatic quatrain. Ogmius was the Celtic god of Gaul (France) identified with Hercules. He was portrayed as an old man with tough skin carrying a bow and club. He was also, strangely, the god of eloquence, and in this capacity he was represented as drawing behind him a company of men whose ears were chained to his tongue.

There is a carved version of Ogmius in the Muse Granet in Aix-en-Provence, southern France, that was known to Nostradamus. In fact, Ogmius was altogether familiar to our prophet historian.

So, first step: we have a god of eloquence and strength as our leading clue. Next we come to "Selin." Selene was the Greek personification of the Moon as a goddess. She was worshipped at the new and full moons. Her parents were Hyperion and Theia; her brother Helois, the sun god, and her sister Eos, who was dawn. Her husband was Zeus, the chief of the gods. Her fame as goddess of the Moon is carried forward to today and reflected in the contemporary goddess movement.

But who did she represent for Nostradamus? Who was this "Moon who will do more?"

We know that it is a "he:" "He will extend his sign to Italy, and will counteract through prudence." The word "sign" in this context means teaching or message. So he will bring his message to counteract whatever ill is occurring in Italy, and he will do this through prudence.

In the majority of the famous interpretations of Nostradamus, this quatrain is associated with the coming of the third Antichrist and some terrible war that will occur in Italy. But here we are convinced of an alternative interpretation.

As we shall learn in the coming chapter concerned with religious change, there is another individual to whom Nostradamus appears to refer in relation to the Moon. He is a religious leader whose people are already present within Italy. In fact, one of them was allegedly murdered by the Mafia in Sicily during 1990 for daring to speak out against them.

This man's name is Osho (originally Rajneesh). Rajneesh means "God of the Moon." The religious upheaval that will occur during the last years of this millennium with the transformation of the Catholic Church will be counteracted by the presence of a new philosophy brought by, perhaps amongst others, the people of this religious leader within Italy. Osho was well known for his eloquence and his strength, chaining the ears of his disciples to his tongue.

As in all matters concerned with religious changes in the world, we are not suggesting that one single individual will undertake such mammoth changes, but that the quatrains indicate certain influences that will help to alter mankind's attitudes towards his gods.

In this quatrain we have interpreted the Moon to indicate a religious concept through the teaching of one man. However, the crescent moon also indicates the Muslim world, so that we may be looking at a new influence from the Middle East toward Italy instead.

Above ~ *the Moon card from the Cary-Yale Scapini tarot deck*

Opposite ~ *a 17th century illustration of the ancient Britain, Ogmius, which Nostradamus uses to indicate his coded message of peace to Italy. Ogmius was said to lead his followers with his great eloquence.*

Italy or the Middle East?

1994 - GADDAFI AWAKENS

WE MENTIONED IN THE LAST PIECE regarding Italy that the Pluto transit through Scorpio and Sagittarius would affect the country in certain ways, but there is also some indication, astrologically, that the Middle East may be an alternative area for conflict during the same periods of the future.

The transiting Mercury/Mars conjunction in Pisces also conjuncts transiting Saturn, that moves into Pisces during 1994, with Mercury going retrograde in Pisces in the same year in February, thus adding power to this astrological lineup. To Nostradamus there would have been a definite element of war in these aspects, because there is a degree of violence in them. But the transiting group does not actually hit Italy's chart.

Mercury governs travel and communications, and this kind of astrological picture can also reflect air crashes, freeway pile-ups and similar accidents, that very often, strangely, seem to happen in groups. In this respect Libya has its Sun in 19 degrees Capricorn, that is being ploughed into by transiting Uranus and Neptune during the first publication of this book – 1993-1994. A likely candidate is Colonel Gaddafi, silent now for some time, but awakened once more during this period to bring troubles to the already troubled Middle East.

Italy has always been the European country at greatest risk from Middle East conflicts because of its geographical location. Gaddafi caused major problems in the Mediterranean during the mid-1980s and has been largely quiet and cooperative since then. The indications from Nostradamus are that he will awaken again during 1994/5 and once more make problems for the world, through some contact with Italy. As though the Middle East needed further problems, with Hussein still active and likely problems in Israel.

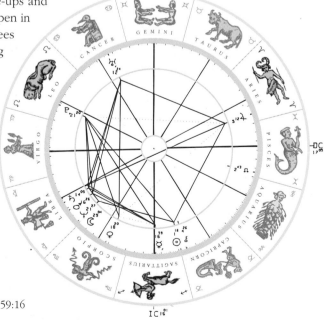

LIBYA

Date: December 24 1951 ❖ Time: 0:00 ❖ Place: Tripoli
Long: 13e11' ❖ Lat: 32n 54' ❖ GMT: 22:00 ❖ Sidereal Time: 4:59:16

SCANDINAVIAN EUROPE

EASTERN
EUROPE

EUROPEAN COMMUNITY

Pressure from Fundamentalist Arab World

MIDDLE EAST

Migrations from Africa

LIBYA

Pressure from Libya & North Africa

Switzerland ~ The End of Neutrality

2000 – SWISS FRANC SWALLOWED UP

Switzerland has always been the bastion of honor, security and a conservative freedom. But the prophet tells us that this story is soon to be over, with financial scandals, political changes and the lifting of the banking secrecy that has hitherto guarded many thousands of accounts against the investigation of police forces and tax authorities across the globe.

Many of the difficulties will arise out of an eventual desire on the part of the country's population to become part of the European Community, though in the mid-1990s there is still little sign of that. By the end of the millennium the interest will have increased, and then the problems of the country will really start.

AKE GENEVA was Nostradamus' focal point for predictions related to Switzerland. There are a number of verses that point us in this direction by referring to "Lac Léman," the early name for the Lake. The Swiss quatrains are amongst the most enigmatic as they contain a number of words that have caused interpreters some problems: words such as "EIOVAS" and "RAYPOZ," that appear at first glance to mean nothing at all except in the mind of Nostradamus himself.

If we look at these bizarre quatrains as a group we find that the Swiss people and their hitherto well-guarded, financially wealthy country must pass through a period of extreme problems at the end of this millennium before entering a greater time of peace and prosperity once again in the new century, as part of the European Community. These problems certainly involve the banking and financial community of the country and are related to financial scandals and the lifting of banking secrecy that has prevailed in this tiny country for so long.

Prés du Leman la frayeur sera grande,
Par le consil, cela ne peut faillir:
Le nouveau Roy fait apprester sa bande,
Le jeune meurt faim, poeur fera faillir.
Presage 4, February.

"Near to Leman (Geneva) fear will be great, by the council (European Community), that does not wish to fail, the new King (process) prepares his design, the young murder hunger, and fear will break."

This verse tells us a general story about the changes facing Switzerland. Put simply, great fear arises in the country because of the coming

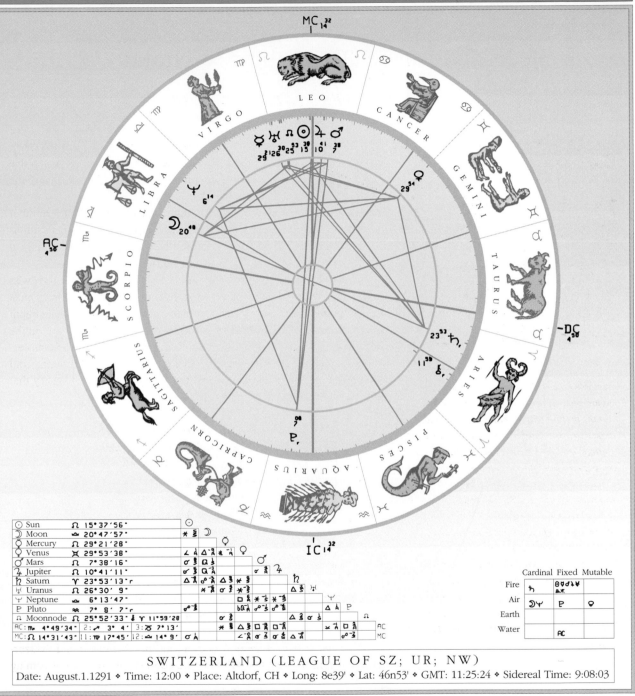

☉ Sun	♌ 15°37'56"	
☽ Moon	♎ 20°47'57"	
☿ Mercury	♌ 29°21'28"	
♀ Venus	♓ 29°53'38"	
♂ Mars	♌ 7°38'16"	
♃ Jupiter	♌ 10°41'11"	
♄ Saturn	♈ 23°53'13" r	
♅ Uranus	♌ 26°30'9"	
♆ Neptune	♎ 6°13'47"	
♇ Pluto	♒ 7°8'7" r	
☊ Moonnode	♌ 25°52'33" ☋ ♈ 11°59'28"	
AC: ♏ 4°49'34"	2: ♐ 3°4' 3: ♑ 7°13'	
MC: ♌ 14°31'43"	11: ♍ 17°45' 12: ♎ 14°9'	

	Cardinal	Fixed	Mutable
Fire	♄	☉♂♃♅☊	
Air	☽☊♆	♇	♀
Earth			
Water		AC	

SWITZERLAND (LEAGUE OF SZ; UR; NW)
Date: August.1.1291 ✦ Time: 12:00 ✦ Place: Altdorf, CH ✦ Long: 8e39' ✦ Lat: 46n53' ✦ GMT: 11:25:24 ✦ Sidereal Time: 9:08:03

The Swiss gold exchange at Credit Suisse bank in Zurich.

One of the major features of Switzerland's future, according to Nostradamus, lies in the power of youth. Young people will have a greater say in the way the country changes.

of a general need to enter the rest of Europe. The European Community "does not wish to fail," and there is much to be lost in Switzerland once it gives up its independence from the rest of Europe. We may have noticed during the early years of the 1990s that Switzerland began its journey through a financial transformation with its own signs of corruption and financial scandal. This is evidently the beginning of something that will grow more serious during the last years of the decade.

Nostradamus often uses the word "King" simply to denote an important process, in this case a design for change that has some connection with the young and their desire for something new – their hunger is murdered and their fear broken. It sounds almost as though the young will direct the way the country alters from its present "perfection" and order to something perhaps a little more exciting and burgeoning.

Eiovas proche esloigner, lac Léman,
Fort grands apprest, retour, confusion:
Loin des Nepveu, de feu grand Supelman,
Tous de leur fuyte.
C12 69

"Eiovas near (or Jupiter approaches) to the area of Lake Leman, big
and strong preparations return, confusion: as far as Nepveux a
great fire Supelman, all vanishing."

This is classic Nostradamus, leaving us apparently with plenty of room to maneuver but in fact, when we get into the detail, very little room at all. There are two choices for the word "Eiovas." It could either be "Savoy" spelled backwards or "Iovis," the Roman god Jupiter. The reference to Savoy would make some sense because the House of Savoy was close to Geneva, but why would Nostradamus need to repeat himself? The reference to Jupiter would seem more useful insofar as Jupiter's passing each year relates in astrological terms to expansion of the economy and in other areas, and Switzerland seems to be due for some changes in its general economic and political situation. The British came out of a Jupiter/Saturn contact (an opposition between transiting Jupiter and transiting Saturn) in 1989-1991, and had to deal with the consequences left in its wake, with a painful and lasting recession. The "mistakes" were made and the seeds sown during the transit, and the consequences were paid for at its end.

The likely transit for Switzerland occurs in the spring of the year 2000 when Jupiter is in Taurus, and the Swiss Sun for the natal chart founded on the ancient "Everlasting League" of the cantons of Schwyz, Uri and Nidwelden and the "new" Constitution of the Federal Republic, is in Leo. The Jupiter transit in 2000 will therefore form a difficult angle (square) to the Swiss Sun. The chart for the birth of the Swiss franc, bastion of world currencies, in fact has its Sun in Taurus, so that this would reflect the same difficulties that we hear from Nostradamus concerning the beginning of a new era when the Swiss franc becomes embroiled within the monetary system of the European Community.

We hear next from Nostradamus that there is the traditional amount of "grands apprest, retour, confusion." – all very characteristic of the prophet's view of changes. The geographical area in question is further defined by more riddles: "Loin des Nepveu..." Interpreters have inferred this to obscure references related to Germany or simply taken the letter "p" out and translated the word to mean nephew, but here again there is a historical interpretation staring us in the face from our French history books.

During the reign of Francis I, when Nostradamus was a young man, a builder by the name of Pierre Nepveu (1519-1547) built one of the finest examples of Renaissance style chateau in France, near the river Loire. This magnificent structure was Francis I's hunting lodge in Chambord, only a few hundred miles from Lake Geneva (Léman), and named Chateau de Chambord.

So, we have our time and we have our place. It seems that an area from Switzerland across to the Loire valley will be touched by these dramatic changes. The only word left in the verse that we have not uncovered the meaning of is "Supelman." The interpreter Edward Leoni puts this down as a possible "superman" and tells us that the word existed in old French.

This doesn't much help us to make complete sense of the verse unless we are dealing with a specific individual yet to appear on the Swiss scene.

Migrés, migrés de Genéve trestous,
Saturne d'or en fer se changera:
Le contre Raypoz exterminera tous
Avant l'advent le ciel signes fera.
C9 44

"Leave, leave Geneva everyone. Saturn will change from gold into iron. Raypoz will kill all who go against him. Before the event there will be signs in the sky."

If we apply this verse to the 21st century evolution of Switzerland, and there are some who would say this is not truly its purpose, then we have to take a quick look at Nostradamus' contemporary attitude to the area.

Geneva was known during Nostradamus' life as the Protestant Rome. John Calvin (1509-1564) built the Protestant Church there and acted as one of the most powerful influences within Protestantism both in Europe and eventually in North America. The Protestant Church was effectively the beginning of the end of the Catholic monopoly in the Western world and therefore the cause of much disturbance. Nostradamus pretended to hate Calvin, being a good converted Catholic himself, so that many of the quatrains concerning Geneva at that time an independent state may have some direct significance to historical times closer to Nostradamus' own life.

The word "Raypoz" more than likely derives from "Zopyra", that is the word turned almost backwards. Zopyra may not sound any more sensible than Raypoz until we discover that it has a historical source.

Zopyra, or Zopyro, was originally a Persian noble who cut off his

Top opposite ~ In the same way as it is possible to have a birth chart for a country, it is also possible to have a birth chart for a commodity such as money, in this case the Swiss Franc, which demonstrates the exact same problems as the natal chart for Switzerland itself.
Bottom opposite and below *~ John Calvin, the religious leader whom Nostradamus often used to denote the region around Geneva, for this was where he set up his center in Europe for the new Protestant Church.*

Jupiter/Saturn conjunctions, such as the one that will occur in Taurus in the spring of 2000 for the Swiss, were consider to be harbingers of the death of a ruler in Nostradamus' time. Both President Lincoln and President Sadat of Egypt were assassinated during such conjunctions. The main picture opposite shows the actual moment of Sadat's assination.

nose and ears pretending to be a fugitive of his own Persian army and assassinated the Babylonian leaders to deliver their army into the hands of King Darius. Philip II of Spain, who vowed to destroy Calvin's Protestant Church on behalf of the Holy Roman Empire, used the sign of Zopyra on one of his battle emblems. It showed two sceptres passed in saltire through a crown over an open pomegranate with the motif, "Tot Zopiro," meaning "as many as Zopyra." The device was said to mean that Philip II wished to have as many faithful subjects as strong and good as Zopyra as there are seeds in a pomegranate.

So, what does all this sophistication actually mean? When we cut out the drama that Nostradamus loved to inject into many of his verses (the poetic license at work), we find three basic subjects:

1. The changing of gold into iron. This process, were it possible, would be the reverse of the alchemical process familiar to Nostradamus – the changing of base metal into gold, largely an allegorical transformation applicable to mankind's evolutionary development from crude matter into god. In this we can read that Switzerland's hitherto financial success, the golden age of the Swiss, may deteriorate.

2. That a powerful figure or, more likely, a series of events, will cause this to come about through a connection with the transformation of independent Switzerland into a part of the European Community, that to many Swiss is enough to cause them to migrate.

3. There will be some astrological forewarning, such as the presence of a Jupiter/Saturn conjunction in Taurus in the spring of 2000. In Nostradamus' time, Jupiter/Saturn conjunctions were also interpreted to mean the death of a ruler and the beginning of a new reign, reflecting the mythic overthrow of Saturn, king of the gods, by his son Jupiter. This conjunction occurred, for example, when Abraham Lincoln was assassinated, and also when President Sadat of Egypt was assassinated. In the case of Switzerland it may be applied to the death of a particular kind of government rather than a single leader.

A Pagan Germany

En Germaine naitront diverses sectes,
S'approchant fort de l'heureux paganisme,
Le coeur captif et petites receptes,
Feront retour a payer le vrai dime.
C3 76

"In Germany will be born different sects, approaching strongly to
happy paganism, the heart captive and receptive to detail, they will
return to pay the true tithe."

OSTRADAMUS HAD A HABIT OF producing these somewhat bizarre verses that manage to create an atmosphere of change without being entirely specific.

The most fascinating thing about this one is that it mirrors almost perfectly, the religious changes that are predicted (Chapter Five) for the end of this century and into the next. Germany, according to these lines, will continue to be a leading nation in terms of social change, insofar as it will allow new ways of thinking and new beliefs to permeate its social awareness. The reference to "happy paganism" is particularly telling as many of the fundamental aspects of the predicted new religious concepts are associated with pre-Christian understanding (Earth-worship, astrological understanding, etc.). There is even a movement already in existence in Germany called the Neo-Pagan Movement, one that originated in the United States. We are told that the "heart (becomes) captive," once again, very much a mirror of the new concept of love that we may see arising in the world after the end of these years of chaos. And finally, "...and receptive to detail." Nostradamus seems to throw this in as a German characteristic! The last line, "...they will return to pay the true tithe..." is a reference to a connection between religion and taxes. We can see this as a pointer to the time when Germany will undertake the changes referred to in the verse.

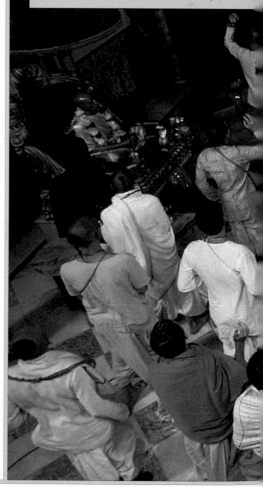

People of the Hare Krishna group gather together for prayer. Nostradamus informs us that Germany will enter a period of the popularity of cult religions and "new age" concepts - a kind of paganism that will transform the country's attitude to the future.

The German Throne of Gold

Aprés viendra des extrême contrées
Prince Germain, dessus le trone doré:
La servitude et eaux rencontrées,
La dame serve, son temps plus m'adoré.

"After there will come from the outermost countries a German Prince, upon the golden throne: the servitude and waters meet, the woman (lady) serves, her time no longer adored."

THE LATE 1980s AND 1990s have seen the German currency rise to the most important level in global economic influence. Economists no longer speak of the dollar or yen but of the German mark as the pointer toward change. The adoption of what was East Germany into the economy has caused considerable impact on the economy of this growing country.

Nostradamus tells us of a German prince who comes from the "outermost countries" to sit upon the "golden throne." The outermost countries are the former East German areas, as we are told that the Prince who comes is already German, not born of any other land. This is a metaphoric reference to the coming of good fortune from the return of a complete Germany following the fall of the Berlin Wall, and the implication is that this "coming home" to the golden throne of Germany is all concerned with the economic growth that is implied in the first two lines. The general indication is that the complete Germany will survive the impact of the "revolution" of the GDR during the coming years.

The third line refers to the meeting of servitude and waters, an astrological reference that brings together the two signs of Pisces and Cancer, though we are not told precisely in what conjunction. The fourth line then continues the astrological story with the "lady serves" indicating the presence of the Moon, "her time no longer adored" implying her waning position. All this gives us a perfect lead into the GDR natal charts.

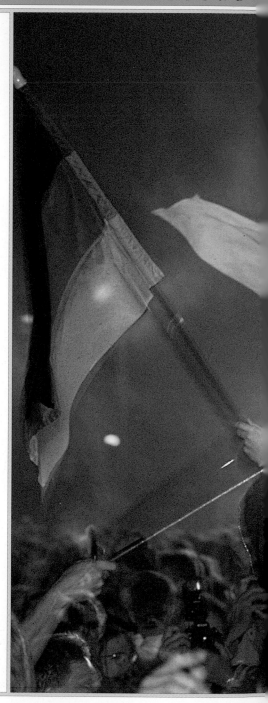

In Berlin on October 3, 1990, a historic evening was shared by all, as the two nations of East and West Germany became one nation. Nostradamus informs us that this new/old country will survive the financial burdens of coming back together again.

GERMAN DEMOCRATIC REPUBLIC

Date: October 7 1949 ❖ Time: 13:30 ❖ Place: Berlin

Long: 13e21' ❖ Lat: 52n29' ❖ GMT: 12:30 ❖ Sidereal Time: 14:26:41

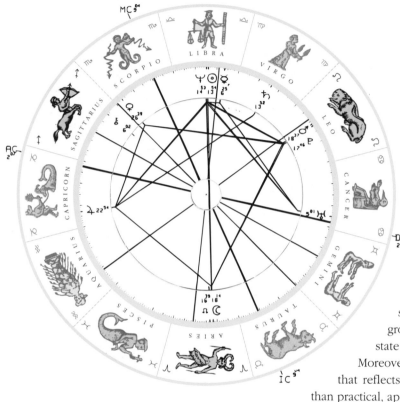

Natal Germany

THE BIRTH CHART for the German Democratic Republic is dated October 7, 1949 at 1:30 p.m. local time, East Berlin. The beginning of the "new life" of Germany from an astrological viewpoint was extremely difficult according to this chart. There is a Sun-Neptune conjunction in the chart, suggesting that a great deal of un-grounded idealism and dreams of a perfect state are part of the nation's psychology. Moreover this conjunction is in the sign of Libra, that reflects an intellectual and idealogical, rather than practical, approach to government. This conjunction is in turn square (a difficult aspect) to the planet Uranus, reflecting a quality of instability and potential for sudden upheaval. It is also opposed to the natal Moon, reflecting a deep dichotomy between the country's conscious ideals and the emotional needs of the people.

The natal chart for the German Democratic Republic indicates that the country was born out of much idealism and little practical good sense. Other characteristics indicate a potential for sudden upheaval and instability. All this seems to have been proven correct.

At the time of the opening of the Berlin Wall, very powerful configurations were occurring in the heavens. The natal chart in this case is begun from November 9, 1989 at 6:57 p.m. local time. A highly unusual exact conjunction of Saturn and Neptune in 10 degrees Capricorn opposed exactly to Jupiter in 10 degrees Cancer is indicated. The

ASTRO-CHART FOR THE OPENING OF THE BERLIN WALL

Date: November 9 1989 ❖ Time: 18:57 ❖ Place: Berlin
Long: 13e21' ❖ Lat: 52n29' ❖ GMT: 17:57 ❖ Sidereal Time: 22:05:56

ascending or rising sign for the GDR chart is in fact Capricorn, and the powerful planetary line-up not only passed over the GDR ascendant, reflecting extreme disruption and change, but also triggered the natal conjunction of Sun-Neptune square Uranus, reflecting instability and the collapse of ideals. The transiting conjunction of Saturn-Neptune in Capricorn, that is a cyclical occurrence happening roughly every 30 years in different signs, heralded to most astrologers some kind of social upheaval since it took place in Capricorn, the sign symbolizing government structures and worldly authority. It is in keeping with the principles of mundane astrology that the particular nation most affected by these deep changes would be one with a Capricorn ascendant, since the ascendant or rising sign reflects the basic personality of the nation. The Moon in the GDR birth chart was also being hit by Saturn and Neptune, reflecting tremendous disillusionment and bitterness rising up within the Eastern German people. No one apparently warned the government what was happening, since such striking aspects require enlightened change, or the result is likely to be revolution.

The birth time for the fall of the Berlin wall brings with it some powerful aspects. Had the rulers of the former East German people taken care to look at their astrology, they might have been able to predict fairly exactly the outcome of their plans.

European Changes

1996 A FRENCH POPE

FRANCE IS, OF COURSE, one of Nostradamus' favorites for prophecy. His love for his own country was set against his irritation for its future and his fear of the consequences of French Revolution and characters such as Napoleon, subjects about which he wrote many verses.

This book would therefore not be complete without some future for France. And we begin with a French Pope.

"Not from Spain but from ancient France one will be elected for the trembling ship, to the enemy will make a promise, who in his reign will cause a terrible plague."

Not so long ago, it would not have been likely that a French Pope could be predicted to ascend the throne of the Catholic Church of Rome. Following Nostradamus' life only Italian Popes succeeded, that is until Pope John Paul II, or Karol Woytijla, the first Polish Pope.

The prophecy at the head of this page makes the picture as clear for us as any could be. There will be the possibility of either a Spanish or a French Pope and the French one will succeed to the "trembling ship," which, as we will see in Chapter Five, is on the cards for the end of this millennium and the early part of the next, when the whole Catholic edifice beings to rock the holy "bark" of Christianity. This new French Pope will make a promise to an enemy. Previous interpreters such as Erica Cheetham have assumed this enemy to be communism, though this seems now to be unlikely unless the Catholic Church is involved with Communist China. It is much more likely that the enemy will be an enemy of the Church itself, an enemy that helps to bring down the ailing clergy. And it is this

Nul de l'Espagne,
Mais de l'antique France
Ne sera lu pour la
Tremblante nacelle,
A l'ennemi sera faite fiance,
Qui dans son regne fera peste cruelle.
C5 49

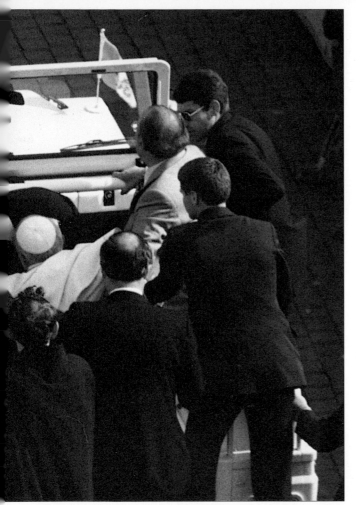

Above ~ *In 1986 the present Pope survived an attempt on his life when he was shot by a would be assassin who claimed he was the reborn Jesus Christ.*

The new French Pope, is to be elected in 1996, after the death of John Paul II, which will occur in the French convent of St. Paul-de-Mausole, where the artist Van Gogh also died.

ailing clergy that we may read into the last part of the prophecy: "...who in his reign will cause a terrible plague." This unfortunate French Pope will be involved in the Church's major problems with AIDS and its effect on the clergy within the hallowed walls of Catholicism. We may therefore date this "French election" to take place very soon after the current Pope's demise, which can be dated according to the previous book in this series in 1995. Given the current increase in the instance of AIDS throughout the world, and the increasing pressure on the Catholic clergy, we could expect a French Pope by 1996.

Within another verse, the story continues:

> *"He (Paul) will die at St. Paul-de-Mausole three leagues from the Rhone, fleeing the two nearest, the tarasca (Mexico) destroyed: for Mars will make the most horrible throne. Of Cock and Eagle of France three brothers."*

Through a complex anagram the Pope's name is given as Paul (John Paul II) and the place of his death at St. Paul-de-Mausole, a convent in France (where Van Gogh committed suicide in 1890). This will occur at a time when the two major powers who are then allies (USA and CIS) will be causing the dying Pope serious problems. Mexico (the Tarascan people live in Mexico) is seriously damaged at that time also, thus giving us greater clues as to the period of the prediction. The Cock is a metaphor for France and the Eagle for the United States. The reference to three brothers is normally interpreted as being the Kennedy brothers (presumably the last remaining), for it turns up in this form in many of Nostradamus' verses. The reference to Mars making the most horrible throne is an astrological clue, as we will now see in our growing jigsaw puzzle surrounding the coming French Pope.

Natal France

According to the French natal chart, France will be clashing frequently with its other European neighbors over the arrangements agreed to in the final EEC treaty.

We have already seen much of the problems that have arisen out of the necessity for all countries to maintain common laws, such as the truckers' strike and blockade of French roads shown opposite on July 4, 1992.

Astrology tells us that these problems will last at least two or three years between 1994 and 1996.

FRANCE HAS UNDERGONE a number of different permutations over the centuries, and is therefore quite difficult to pin down astrologically. Most astrologers have selected the birth of the current regime as the most likely natal point at which to begin the story. This dates it at the Fifth Republic created by General de Gaulle after the failure of the Fourth Republic. The Fifth Republic was born on October 5, 1958, with the legislation coming into affect at midnight *(The Book of World Horoscopes –* Nicholas Campion).

The ascendant for this chart is 24 degrees of Cancer and the first important transit following publication of this book is the joint transit of Uranus and Neptune opposing the French ascendant. Uranus is in exact opposition beginning February 1994, while Neptune reaches this point

in April 1994. Uranus will remain in position until December 1994 and Neptune through 1995 and 1996, completing its passage in November of that year. These transits do not suggest a "fall" or collapse in the structure of government, but they do suggest struggles and disappointments with other countries, as the ascendant/descendant axis is concerned with the relationship of an entity with the "other" – in the case of a nation, other nations.

The French Mars (and this is significant to our verse), which is in 2 degrees of Gemini, is also activated during this period, with transiting Pluto forming an opposition to it ("Mars will make the most horrible throne"). As this French Mars is placed within the natal house concerned with larger groups and organizations, we may justifiably expect some hot moments within the European Community between France and its neighbors. We saw this during 1992 with the French willingness to sabotage the world trade agreement to their own advantage.

The French Sun is placed in 11 degrees of Libra, conjuncting Venus and in trine to Mars. This is a very positive and attractive configuration, suggesting dynamic energy but also willingness to compromise and adjust. However, the transits of Uranus and Neptune to the French ascendant, combined with the French Mars being stirred up so powerfully by Pluto (the house cleaner), all suggest that France's normal diplomatic stance is likely to be temporarily replaced by an angrier and more militant one. These are not warlike configurations, but reflect trouble with neighbors and partners, and an intractable and aggressive attitude which is likely to create great unpopularity over a period of two or three years.

In conclusion we may expect the new French Pope to be involved in the troubles of France in the new European Community during 1995/6, after the death of Pope John Paul II.

Natal Spain

W E ARE CONCERNED WITH two natal charts in relation to Spain. The first, taken from Nicholas Campion's *The Book of World Horoscopes*, is that of the original Spain, formed by the union of Aragon and Castile, set for the day that Juan II of Aragon died, January 19, 1479, on which day the succession was effectively granted to Ferdinand of Aragon. The chart is set for Madrid without a recorded birth time, though Nicholas Campion takes 12 noon local mean time.

This chart has the Sun in 8 degrees Aquarius, in harmonious aspect to the natal Pluto. The intensity, determination and self-regeneration capacities of Spain are reflected by this configuration. The natal Moon is in 28 degrees of Sagittarius, reflecting the expansionist and deeply religious temperament which made Spain create a religious and economic empire in the New World. There is also a quality of great resilience and perennial faith in the future reflected by this natal Moon in Sagittarius, and Spain's remarkable regeneration since Juan Carlos took the throne in 1975 is testimony to this. Any temporary government would be underpinned by these basic Spanish characteristics.

There are no particularly heavy transits occurring across this chart during the latter part of the 20th century. Uranus enters Aquarius in April 1995, and reaches a conjunction with the Spanish Sun in April/May 1997. It remains here until October 1998. This is disruptive and suggests change, but not of a serious or threatening nature, most likely a new outlook which involves territory in relation to the Basque people. Transiting Pluto will eventually reach the Spanish Sun when it transits through Aquarius, making the exact conjunction during 2028/2029. This would indicate a profound change in some major aspect of the country's structure, perhaps involving government.

The chart for the coronation of Juan Carlos, however, is more striking in terms of transits. This is the current chart for Spain, set for November 22, 1975, in Madrid at 12.45 p.m., when the King took the oath of allegiance in Parliament.

Above ~ *Rough seas for the EEC*

This chart has the Sun in 29 degrees Scorpio, and an ascendant in 3 degrees Aquarius, with natal Saturn opposing the ascendant from 2 degrees Leo. This immediately suggests a propensity in the natal chart for trouble with partner nations, and feelings of being restricted or blocked by them. Although Spain is enthusiastic about the EC, it is in fact a country which, under the government in the early 1990s, would fare better with greater autonomy. As transiting Uranus moves into Aquarius, it will reach the Spanish ascendant and oppose the Spanish Saturn from March 1996 through January 1997. Transiting Pluto in the meantime will arrive on the Spanish Sun in December 1994, completing its exact conjunction in November 1995 but continuing to transit close to it until September 1996. This period (1994-1997) overlaps with the transits in the French chart, and it is therefore only possible to conclude that the European process will be going through its problems for those years before settling down into some cooperation. During this time there will be some bitter confrontations between France and Spain.

During 1992, Britain was the problem within the EC, but after 1994 Spain and France will rule the troubled waves of the new European Community.

Examining the two natal charts of France and Spain we begin to see that there are elements in each which indicate problems within the European Community during coming years. Between 1994 and 1997 there will be continual problems within the EEC and Spain will be as much involved in them as France.

It is also indicated that France and Spain will be arguing with each other, over issues involving their relationship within the Community.

Chapter 5
THE TRANSFORMING OF GOD

N THIS CHAPTER WE WILL TAKE A detailed look at the way Nostradamus saw the end of this century as a time when organized religion would undergo major changes. And, as always, we must first go on a quest to open up the flowers of the Master's verses.

L'an mil neuf cent nonante neuf sept mois,
Du ciel viendra un grand Roy d'effrayeur
Ressusciter le grand Roy d'Angoulmois,
Avant apres Mars regner par bonheur.
C10 72

"The year 1999 and seven months, from the skies will come a great and frightening King, to resuscitate the great King of Angoulmois, before after Mars to reign through happiness."

Opposite ~ One of the glittering spires of materialism in Manhattan. Yet, according to Nostradamus, it is New York that will be the center of a major spiritual upheaval connected with a great leader.
Above ~ The young and innocent indoctrinated into belief for the sake of a distant god.

Several interpreters have simply attributed this quatrain to a prediction of the end of the world. It is one of only a few quatrains in *The Centuries* to specifically mention a date in Nostradamus' future. 1999 happens to be a very emotive and provocative year. It is the end of a century, the end of a millennium, and therefore could be seen to be the end of an era, or even the end of mankind.

The Transformation of Catholicism

JULY 1999

THE CONCEPT OF A "DOOMSDAY" is a popular one among many interpreters. But it is likely that the world is not actually going to end in the last year of this millennium. The universe tends not to be aware of mankind's calendars, only mankind is aware of the time of day and the date of the year. Nostradamus was not a fool and would not have made such a presumption. This does not detract, however, from the importance of the whole concept of "the millennium" as a turning point in human transformation.

The first, most important, part of this verse is the reference to "Angoulmois," for this brings us back to our suggestion that many of the prophet's verses contain words that are essentially historically sourced.

Most interpreters take the name "Angoulmois" in relation only to its ancient position in the Dark Ages, so this is where we will begin our hunt.

The people of Angouléme were invaded by the Huns, a Mongol race led by a violent and powerful king named Attila. The area of Angoulmois, that was then the province of France in which the city of Angouléme stood, was a large area of southwest France, now known as Charente. The city lies upon a high plateau above the conjunction of the Charente and Anguienne rivers and was therefore a great vantage point for conquering Visigoths, Huns, and Mongols. But why are we looking at this obscure place in relation to a King hundreds of years before Nostradamus' lifetime?

The popular belief is that there is some connection between the ancient Mongols and the Book of Revelations insofar as Nostradamus appears to make reference to the raising of the dead – "to resuscitate the great King of Angoulmois" – i.e. that the Second Advent will bring Christ back to raise Attila the Hun from his rotting grave and judge him for his dastardly deeds, or something of that kind. This seems somewhat obscure. There may be a much simpler reason for the use of the town as a symbol.

Let's look a little further into the future of Attila the Hun. In fact, let's move right forward to the time of Nostradamus himself.

During Nostradamus' early years, around 1524 when he was 18, a man named Giovanni da Verrazano served the French king Francis I, from 1515-1547. Francis I also happened to be Count of Angouléme, being part of the French royal dynasty of Valois (the same dynasty to which Catherine de Medici belonged).

Verrazano traveled a very long distance to a remote island off the coast of a country that had been visited just 32 years earlier by Columbus. Verrazano called this island Angouléme after his master's title Count of Angouléme. It later became known as Manhattan Island. One of the bridges leading out of Manhattan is named after the island's founder _ Verrazano Bridge.

Nostradamus would have known all about "Angouléme" and if we believe in his powers of "sight" he would have had at least some idea about what this small island was going to turn out to be some years later.

The connections with the Book of Revelations are also traditionally tied together by turning the numbers 999 upside down to make 666 – the sign of the "Beast of the Apocalypse" – the Devil. This may have some significance if we consider how many of the prophet's predictions have a strong flavor of religious doom, but it seems less sensible to worry too much about this.

So, we have a "terrifying" leader likely to appear from the sky in the last year of this century over New York City. In fact, this is supposed to

Opposite ~ King Francis I of France, who was king during the first part of Nostradamus' life, and a sovereign warrior who spent the greater part of his rule fighting the Holy Roman Empire.

Above ~ Giovanni da Verrazano, an Italian within the French court of Francis I who set down on an island near the freshly discovered America, and named it Angouleme after one of Francis' other titles – Count of Angouleme – the same island that would later be named Manhattan Island.

The modern Catholic Church still maintains the same religious trappings that it did in Nostradamus' time. This picture was taken on January 6, 1988, during a papal consecration. Throughout its relatively short career, the Catholic Church has caused more grief, death and destruction than any other organized religion in the history of mankind. Nostradamus and astrology indicate that a major transformation will put an end to this before the century is out.

happen in July 1999. And it would appear to have some direct religious significance. But why? Where is the final link? What does Francis I, king of France during Nostradamus' youth have to do with religion?

The answer lies in the fact that Francis I spent 23 years of his reign, between 1521 and 1544 (while the young Nostradamus grew from 15 to 38), at war with the Holy Roman Empire – fighting against the earthly representative of the Catholic Church.

Now Nostradamus, being a converted Jew, running during much of his life from the dreaded Catholic Inquisition, who wished to "interview" him for a number of insurgences, might well have had much empathy for the attitudes of King Francis I in his battles with the Church. He might, and probably did, look upon Francis as something of a hero – even a "great King." "The Great King of Angouléme (Manhattan)." One who would come from the sky and resuscitate the memory of this great king might be one who would deal the final blow to the Catholic Church at the end of the 20th century.

At time of writing (early 1993) the Papacy is attacking the American bishops for their attitude towards what is judged by the Church to be the "unnatural" behavior of homosexuals within and outside the Church itself. The American Bishops have come under more attack from the Catholic Church than any other of the world diocese. According to Nostradamus this will escalate into a major upheaval during the last year of the millennium and be connected with a great leader (that may be a metaphor for simply a great change, not necessarily involving one person, but a new paradigm engendered by human understanding) who will come to New York and bring a new kind of religion.

The Astrology for July 1999

As is frequently the case, astrological readings and Nostradamus' quantrains coincide almost exactly. The prophet did not often make such strikingly exact predictions, giving year and month in one verse, but the timing of the event so close to the end of a millennium, and the coincidence of an important astrological conjunction must have been dramatic enough for Nostradamus to make so precise a strike at the future.

W E SHOULD REMEMBER AT THIS POINT the astrological background to the period from the first chapter. The Aquarian Age will certainly bring change and in particular a new vision of godliness that will have less to do with blind belief and miracles and more to do with analytical and objective reasoning. A god that can be questioned. And in addition we will see the passing of Pluto the detoxifier through Saggittarius, the sign of religious belief.

July 1999 is the precise date when Jupiter enters Taurus and begins to apply its conjunction with Saturn, that approaches through the rest of 1999 and is exact in the spring of 2000. Nostradamus would have placed great importance on this conjunction occurring simultaneously with the end of the millennium.

If we take a closer look at the natal chart of the Vatican City, based on the Treaty of Lateran on February 11, 1929, a treaty that formalized the present-day boundaries between the Vatican and Italy, we find something very powerful indeed. The chart contains a benign configuration between the Sun in Aquarius and Mars in Gemini that gives great energy and dynamism, and in addition an equally benign aspect between the Sun and Saturn in Sagittarius that gives longevity and stability.

During 1992 the transit of Pluto has been making a square (difficult) to the Sun in this natal chart. All that really happened out of that, apart from the ongoing problems within Catholicism, is that the Pope became ill during that year (except of course, we don't really know what was going on behind the scenes).

However, transiting Uranus will soon arrive in Aquarius and comes up to the natal Sun in May 2000. Nostradamus would not have known about Uranus, but perhaps he relied more upon his clairvoyant gifts for this prediction. The transiting Uranus makes a station there in May, directly on the Vatican Sun, and then remains in that region for the whole of the year 2000 and into 2001, making another station in the same place in October 2001.

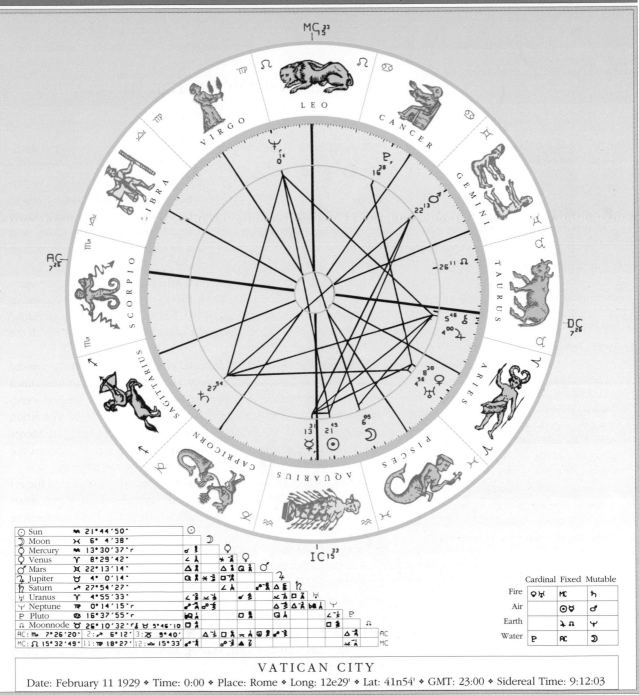

☉ Sun	♒ 21°44'50"	☉							
☽ Moon	♓ 6° 4'38"	☽							
☿ Mercury	♒ 13°30'37" r		♀						
♀ Venus	♈ 8°29'42"								♀
♂ Mars	♓ 22°13'14"								♂
♃ Jupiter	♉ 4° 0'14"								
♄ Saturn	♐ 27°54'27"								
♅ Uranus	♈ 4°55'33"								
♆ Neptune	♏ 0°14'15" r								
♇ Pluto	♏ 16°37'55" r								
☊ Moonnode	♉ 26°10'32" r		☋ 5°46'10						☊
AC: ♏ 7°26'20"	2: ♐ 6°12'	3: ♑ 5°40'							AC
MC: ♌ 15°32'49"	11: ♍ 18°27'	12: ♎ 15°33'							MC

	Cardinal	Fixed	Mutable
Fire	♀ ♅	♏	♄
Air		☉ ☿	♂
Earth		♐ ☊	♆
Water	♇	AC	☽

VATICAN CITY
Date: February 11 1929 ❖ Time: 0:00 ❖ Place: Rome ❖ Long: 12e29' ❖ Lat: 41n54' ❖ GMT: 23:00 ❖ Sidereal Time: 9:12:03

165

When heavy planets make stations, these become powerful nodal points in the overall transit and tend to reflect big events. It would seem likely that Pope John Paul II will not make it through to this date.

It looks very much as though the established Churches may need to rethink their purpose within the next few years.

Nostradamus rarely left a line, even a single word, without some meaning attached to it. As we may by now have realized, this was a brilliant poet at work, but a poet with a considerable knowledge of world events that he applied to the future.

"...before after Mars to reign through happiness."

What has happiness to do with Mars, the god of war? The implication all through this prophecy is that the Catholic Church with its mounting difficulties will be transformed by some powerful individual (or movement) who will be connected with Manhattan Island. To Nostradamus, this might have seemed a happy event. He tells us in passing that Mars still reigns, i.e., wars are still going on in 1999. But we know that is likely anyway. Though one thing that might be remembered is that over the past 3,000 years almost 90 percent of the 5,000 wars that mankind has undertaken have been fought for religious reasons. So wars continue to happen during the happiness engendered by a change in God.

In April 2000 there is a big conjunction of Mars with the transiting Jupiter and Saturn in Taurus (we heard about this in the predictions for Switzerland). This may be applicable to Nostradamus' reference to "before and after" Mars – the period of the Mars involvement with the conjunction really occurs only during April of that year. But these three planets don't usually conjunct at the same time. It is a rarity, and any two in conjunction would, to a Renaissance astrologer, have meant something important. The conjunction falls around the mid-Taurus. This will affect the charts of a number of countries, and it would be impossible astrologically to predict exactly who will do what to whom.

America's chart is not one of these, but in 2000 America has the transit of Pluto beginning across its ascendant in Sagittarius, so we can expect some major changes in the religions of America during such a transit, the character of which follows in this chapter. The Sagittarian ascendant in the American chart reflects a deeply religious spirit in America, that will come out in a rather "cranky" or fanatical fashion as part of the ceaseless Sagittarian quest for enlightenment.

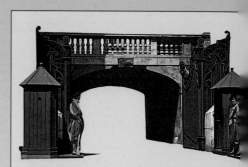

Above *~ The Arch of the Campane guarded by the famous Swiss guards provided by the Swiss a. the most celebrated addition to Vatican security.*
Right *~ The Dome of St. Peter's constructed from a drawing by Michelangelo which had been inspired by the dome of Santa Maria del Fiore in Florence.*

The New God across Europe

1995 – THE FALL OF CATHOLICISM

De Fez le regne parviendra à ceux d'Europe,
Feu leur cité et lame trenchera:
Le grand d'Asie terre et mer à grand troupe,
Que peur bleux, croix, a mort dechassera.
C6 80

"From Fez (Morocco) the reign will reach to those of Europe, fire their city and cut decisively: The great one of Asia by land and sea a large group, the cross that has scared stiff will be driven out to death."

NCE AGAIN HERE, we have a perfect example of a quatrain that has been interpreted up until now according to a war-like consciousness. The words in the second line, "Feu leur cit et lame trenchera," have been generally translated to mean, "The city blazes, the sword will slash..." Naturally, if we come to Nostradamus expecting war, we will translate his verse in this way. However, if we alter our consciousness to a more peaceful mode, we get something quite different.

A city that is fired can be a city that is inspired rather than actually burning. Instead of "swords slashing," the French words "lame trenchera" can better mean "cut decisively."

The words, "grand troupe," from a warrior standpoint would naturally mean a big army, but if we drop the sword we can also drop the army that carries it, so that the words can then simply mean a "large group."

And finally, the most common representation of the last line of this

Sooner or later the romance of the Catholic Church will be outweighed by its evident archaicism. Blind faith was created to drive people out of their suffering and into obedience to the state and to God.

But as humans become more intelligent and less frightened, they begin to see more

romance and less suffering in a god that is closer to home. Heaven is out, the individual spirit and a resident godliness is in during the last few years of the 20th century.

By the 21st century god will mean something completely different.

quatrain is, in the French, "Que bleux, pers, croix, à mort dechessera." This seems to make no sense at all unless we take the word "pers" and make it into a future individual (a common device with interpreters when they don't know the meaning of a word), perhaps the third Antichrist who will have the name Pers. Once again a complicated and war-like interpretation. All we need to do is look up in the French dictionary and we find that "peur bleux" means "scared stiff," or literally "frightened blue." "Que peur bleux, croix, a mort dechassera." "This very frightened cross will be driven out to death."

So, from being a verse depicting terrible war and death by fire, we have a verse that tells of the spread of a new religion, once again involving influence from Asia with a large group of people who go from Morocco across Europe and inspire the cities with the decisiveness of the new understanding of religion, frightening the Christian cross to death.

Nostradamus' vision knocks down the old. But it also gives birth to the new. Human changes tend to happen quite slowly – particularly in areas of major importance like war or religious belief. In the same way as the Aquarian Age passes through hundreds of years of transformation from the Piscean Age, so the new understanding of God will undergo its transformation slowly. In fact, the changes that can be foreseen for the next millennium have already begun in this millennium. And there are plenty of hints from the master of prophecy. There are a number of quatrains that give us a picture of the way our religious future will unfold. These include both the philosophy behind the changes and the individuals who are or have been part of the influence for change.

Porphyry Rocks the Boat

OR THOSE WHO HAVE LIVED the whole of their lives in either the shadow or the light of the Christian Church, it may be difficult to imagine that there could be anything else as a main religious force in the Western world. But Christianity is a relatively young belief system, and Nostradamus gives us hints periodically that we may be turning toward something based in a much older form of belief.

Avant qu'avienne le changement d'Empire,
Il aviendra un cas bien merveilleux:
Le champ mué, le pilier de porphyry
Mis, translaté sus le rocher noueux.
C1 43

Porphyry reflected the anti-Christian views of the first century after Christ. At that time the Christian faith was largely a cult like any modern cult that attracts society's disapproval. No one knew much about Jesus nor cared, until almost four hundred years after his death, when a Roman Emperor rescuscitated the reputation of someone he knew almost nothing about. Even the great passages of the Bible were written by men who never met Jesus. And it is this that we have based the Christian religions on.

"Before the change of Empire happens, a very marvelous example will occur: the field (area) moved, the mainstay (pillar or tree) of porphyry placed, transferred onto the gnarled rock."

As we have seen within many of the interpretations of the prophetic verses, Nostradamus liked to make use of famous individuals from his own past or present to illustrate his meanings. These names are mostly completely unknown to 20th-century man, as they have disappeared into history within the dusty volumes of libraries. One of these names is the neoplatonist Greek philosopher Porphyry, for example. Who would know such a name today? Yet it is written, plain and simple, within the lines of this verse.

Porphyry was an anti-Christian (then known as the new religion) philosopher living between the years CE 234 and 305 in Rome, right at the very start of the Church to be attributed to Jesus Christ. His book *Against the Christians* was ceremoniously burned in 448, though his attitudes remained alive certainly into the time of Nostradamus, as he was particularly famous for his writings on Aristotle that set the stage for medieval logic.

Amongst his basic ideas, Porphyry was particularly keen on vegetarianism, and in medieval textbooks the "Porphyrian Tree" was used as a basis for understanding logic classifications of the substance of life, of which abstinence and vegetarianism were basic. All this would have been entirely familiar to Nostradamus, who is telling us that shortly before the whole Christian edifice is transformed an example of the new form of religion will occur in a "marvelous" way: "...the field (area or concept) moved, the mainstay (pillar or tree) of porphyry placed, transferred onto the gnarled rock."

The "gnarled rock" is of course the rock of St. Peter in Rome, the Catholic Church, gnarled from being beaten.

Honey & Wax

Not satisfied with this eccentric and delightful piece of poetic prophecy, our 16th-century genius goes still further in the very next verse, continuing his descriptive story.

"In short there will be the return of sacrifices, transgressors will be put to martyrdom: no longer will there be monks, priests or novices: honey will be more expensive than wax."
C1 44

A SHORT TIME AFTER THE "new religion" has taken hold, as with all religions in the past, the people, the followers, the new "converts" will start to punish those who don't believe. The foolishness of some members of the human race will not end with a transformation of the Church. The martyrdom may not contain the same degree of violence that existed in Nostradamus' time, but this is the way he would have seen the potential future in a radical new religious climate, projected from the horrors of the Spanish Inquisition and all the religious turmoil that was part of his daily life.

On the other hand, we in the 20th century are not exactly free from horrors, either religious or otherwise, and a new reformed religiousness has the same potential for disaster as any previous one – particularly given the human tendency to destroy innocence and joy.

The monks, priests, and novices in their original form, will be gone. This much he makes patently clear. And, finally, honey will be more expensive than wax. Put another way, the old crusty clerical wax used for candles and for church bureaucracy will disappear in favor of the pure diet, the healthy presence of natural foods.

Our picture of the new way grows steadily. It contains purer attitudes (though not puritan) of diet and health. Vegetarianism will be a part of the story, and the priests and monks will be transformed or entirely absent. Perhaps now we can search for clues to see if there is an indication about the basis for the new religiousness.

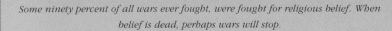

Some ninety percent of all wars ever fought, were fought for religious belief. When belief is dead, perhaps wars will stop.

The Man of Ornate Speeches

Celuy qu'aura la charge de destruire
Temples & sectes changes par fantasie,
Plus aux rochers qu'aux
Vivans viendra nuyre,
Par langue ornee d'oreilles ressaisies.
C1 96

"He that will have the responsibility to break down temples and sects altered through fantasy, will come to harm more the rocks than the living, through ornate language ears will continuously be filled."

History has invariably provided us with pointers toward change. As an age of crisis appears, so the pointers increase in number. During the time of Buddha there were no less than 11 enlightened masters of at least the stature of Jesus, in the Far East. During the latter years of this century, at a time when crisis seems to dominate life, there have been more powerful religious voices sounding from India than for many centuries. This is a time of massive transformation for the human heart.

Above ~ *A Bodhisattva, probably of the Sui Dynasty, combining Indian mysticism and classical beauty of form.*

Opposite ~ *A black marble sculpture of Buddha.*

INTERPRETERS OF NOSTRADAMUS have related this verse to the arrival of a religious leader who will be more concerned with people than temples. The buildings that have exemplified organized religion so far in past religious beliefs are already deteriorating in parts of Europe, particularly England, where many churches have either collapsed through lack of interest or are being converted into homes or offices.

It is suggested by past interpreters that the mention of the "rock" refers perhaps to the rock of St. Peter – the Vatican or Catholic Church. The conclusion therefore is that this man's powerful capabilities as a religious leader will do harm to Catholicism. This seems all quite logical, and most of the more intelligent interpretations the story is agreed on.

But there is more here than at first meets the eye, and if we take out our detective's magnifying glass we begin to see some of the ideas that

Nostradamus had about this man (or influence), written between the lines.

In this chapter of the book we are not in any way suggesting that any single individual will lead the world into some mighty new way of being, for, as we have seen in early interpretations, the intention is to suggest that mankind himself will make the changes necessary for a greater fulfillment in life and a happier future. But perhaps there are major influences that began at the hands of particular people who are indicated by the quatrains. In fact, the impression from reading Nostradamus is that the transformation will occur through a change in attitude in us, but that guidance may be sought from some rather special people. In fact, for the purposes of illustrating the concepts of the new religiousness, we will use two well-known personalities, one of whom is frequently referred to in the quatrains. The other will serve to help us understand something of the central issues that will perhaps touch our attitudes towards god in the future. There have been, in addition to these two individuals, many others such as Buddha, Mahavira, Lao Tzu, as well as Muslim leaders and a general sense of the presence of the East, all of which have contributed to the changes that we may expect to discover during the turn of the centuries. The problem with attempting to explain the religious changes that are suggested by Nostradamus is that they are essentially largely unfamiliar to the western mind and therefore all we can do is give some direction by using the example of individuals about whom the reader can find further reading.

We will start with the Eastern influence, and the man Nostradamus seems to indicate has given us some indication of the ground for our religious future.

Lord of the Full Moon

HE FIRST SIGNIFICANT WORDS in the quatrain above are "...altered through fantasy." It seems as though this might be a hint as to the qualities of the attitudes we are looking for. It could be construed that human fantasy has altered the original message of the Catholic Church, but a better word to use to describe this change would perhaps be dogma or fear or any number of words other than fantasy. So perhaps the word more readily describes the source of the vision that comes to change our lives so dramatically.

The next most significant line is "will come to harm more the rocks than the living..." This man is a man of love. Therefore, he is a man that is concerned with humanity and not the edifices, the golden cows, that man tends to erect when there is no real religious guidance available. This sounds a little like Jesus – the man that smashed the temples and pulled down the old ideas – a man of true vision.

And third comes the line: "...through ornate language ears will continuously be filled." This is a man of speeches, a man, what's more, of beautiful words that will continuously fill the ears of those that listen.

If we accept the dating in the first quatrain of this chapter – i.e., that this new religious influence will be felt in the latter part of the 1990s and that it will coincide with the transformation of the Catholic Church (remember that astrologically this is due to begin happening when Pluto enters Saggitarius after 1995), then we can presume that the character Nostradamus is using to give us hints about the new ideas of god is already very much in evidence. He must also be a highly significant person, a powerful religious leader who would have sufficient influence to make such an impact. It seems also from the first line of the quatrain that he was at some time charged with actually destroying the temples of the establishment. Perhaps even imprisoned.

Also, as a final clue, Nostradamus does not tell us in this second verse that the man is necessarily alive or dead.

Perhaps we need to look elsewhere for another verse to give us further clues.

Above ~ The Moon personified, with the image of the astrological sign of Cancer between her legs, over which she rules. At the bottom of the picture lies the sea, over which she has total domain.

For clues to our future religious beliefs we must measure Nostradamus' verses against the ancient mythology he sews into the words. If we search like detectives we find a great number of directions, both subtle and obvious, that show us the way to a new attitude that has to do with an intensely personal view of life and death, but little or nothing to do with outmoded rites and rules.

There are a series of verses in the second *Century* that may help us. Some of Nostradamus' verses are very hard to pin down. There is often no specific word or phrase that can give us sound clues for our progress, but these particular verses abound with goodies!

> *"The penultimate name of the prophet takes Diana for his day and rest: wandering far (or from a long way off) with loose-fitting robe through an infuriating testament, and deliver a great people from imposition (taxation in old French)."*

As is often the case in translation, Nostradamus' verses don't necessarily string together in perfect English, but it seems better to translate literally rather than putting words into the master's mouth as so many interpreters have in the past. So, what does this verse reveal? The last but one name of this religious guide to our future will have something to do with Diana. Might this be Diana, the goddess of the Moon?

Second, the man seems to come from a long way off and wears loose-fitting robes, though the word "vaguera" could also mean "far away." It seems unlikely that Nostradamus would have used the words "far away" twice in "Loing" and "vaguera." So coming from far away and wearing loose-fitting robes gives us some very precise clues.

He offers this "infuriating" testament and delivers many people from imposition – the imposition, no doubt in Nostradamus' mind, of the established religions.

Other quatrains also suggest that he came from the East, so that our clue that he is far away seems to point towards India, if we also take into account clue 12 (see box) for in India, cremation is the most common form of burial.

We can now pinpoint a single individual whom Nostradamus may have been pointing to to indicate to us the kind of philosophy that will provide us with a new religious concept. Though, once again, it is emphasized that the author's intention is not to suggest that this or any other single individual will become a replacement for any of the existing Churches, for this would be entirely against the indications from both Nostradamus and the astrological implications for the period.

The new religiousness will have to do with self-knowledge, with a new type of love, with personal power, joy and more than all these things, with meditation.

In the West, meditation is thoroughly misunderstood, for we still believe that it is not possible to stop thinking. We think that thought is everything. In the East, thought is nothing. It is considered second best.

So, let us sum up our clues:
1. A man of fantasy.
2. A man who advocates love and iconoclasm.
3. A man of poetry to whom people listen.
4. We probably already know about him.
5. He may have been charged and even imprisoned for his "infuriating" message.
6. He maybe alive or dead.
7. Last but one name has something to do with Diana, possibly the Moon.
8. He comes from far away.
9. He probably wears loose-fitting robes.

10. He delivers an infuriating testament, perhaps thereby getting into trouble. (See also clue 5 above) And further clues:

*"His disciples invite him to become immortal...
His body in the fire."*

There are also various references to the Moon and this man being "alone with his mind" and "silent in rest."

These perhaps provide the final necessary answers to our quest.
11. This man is already dead.
12. His body was cremated.

Rajneesh Chandra Mohan

Osho, a man who recently left his body, but who while on this planet brought one of the best examples of how to live with joy and meditation as a practical reality.

Nostradamus used this man as one of the keys to tell us how to open the door to the future of love.

I N A PREVIOUS BOOK ABOUT Nostradamus' prophecies (*Nostradamus – The End of the Millennium*), V.J.Hewitt created a complex coding system to decode the prophet's quatrains. Whatever the merits may have been of using this method, it revealed a name, purely through the use of numerology and anagram, that is the same name to be indicated by our detective work in this chapter. In a still earlier book, written by John Hogue in the mid-1980s, the same name turned up yet again as the likely man whose ideas and philosophies might help engender a major religious change at the end of this century.

Let us measure our clues against this man.

1. His name was originally Rajneesh Chandra Mohan. He was a professor of philosophy in India until the early 1970s when he began teaching to large audiences a new way of looking at religion and personal belief that was considered highly original and very different from the established concept of religion taught within the established churches. He was also very scathing about these religions and spoke with great fantasy and poetry.

The second to last name, Chandra, means Moon. The name Rajneesh means "Lord of the Full Moon." This seems to satisfy clues number 1, 2, 3, and 7.

2. During the 1970s he lived and spoke to thousands of disciples and visitors at the Rajneesh Ashram in Poona, India. Here he continued to upset the authorities with his highly controversial and "infuriating" discourses. On several occasions the Indian authorities attempted to stop his work, and the extent of his influence stretched even to America and Europe as he spoke about President Reagan and the Pope with very little sympathy or support. This seems to satisfy clues number 4 and 8.

3. When coming to discourses within the ashram, Rajneesh always

Osho, the Indian Master who led the way to one of the most revolutionary new views of religiousness to be available to the West this century.

wore long, loose-fitting robes. Clue number 9.

4. In 1981 he departed India for America. During the four years that he was there he spoke continuously against the US government and was eventually forced to leave due to the alleged crimes of a small number of his disciples. Before being permitted to return to India, he was imprisoned in South Carolina and then in Oregon and charged with illegal residence in the US. Although the charges were dropped, he was forced to leave the country. It is generally believed that he was forced to leave simply because of his "infuriating testimony." Clues 5 and 10 satisfied.

5. After leaving the US he was refused permission to stay in most of the "civilized" countries of the world. During a long period of touring from one place to another, it appeared that no country was willing to allow him to continue his "infuriating testimony." It seemed almost as though the whole world was afraid of the truth that this man wished to tell.

He eventually returned to India and the ashram was reopened in Poona, a large city near Bombay. Shortly after this he changed his name to Osho. In January 1990 he died. After his death, his disciples performed the traditional Indian method of burning his body to ashes. Clues 6, 11, and 12 seem satisfied by this.

The rest of the centuries quatrains are peppered with other clues that make it hard to place any other name at the head of the list for a single individual whose teaching can provide us with a guide to the direction for our global religious ideas in the future.

The most interesting thing about all these indicators is that each one signifies something greater than the individual man. There is a general series of hints that show us the way towards concepts involving the East, reincarnation, love, the inner journey, and meditation, and we may read into this what Nostradamus was attempting to provide as a potential new direction.

C.G. Jung
The Spirit of the West

HE EASTERN INFLUENCE may seem to be a vital aspect of our future religious beliefs, but we can also take a look at another character who will have some influence on our spiritual future. C.G. Jung is perhaps more familiar to Western minds of the late 20th century than Osho, but his message is essentially the same, though expressed through a more Western approach. We have used Nostradamus' predictions to indicate a direction of religious change from the East. We will now use astrology as the method to get a better look at the character of this religion from the more familiar angle of the western mind by taking the natal chart of C.J.Jung.

As a first point, no birth chart can fully reflect the degree of talent, vision, or stature of any individual. This seems to be a quality of "soul" that is not mapped by the natal horoscope. The chart reflects the nature of the personality and the likely channels through which talents are likely to be expressed. So there may be many charts similar to those of our chosen characters, but these people express their similar personality qualities in less global terms. There is a famous example of this given in the book *The Case for Astrology* of a man born on the same day as King George VI. He was a shoemaker. He married on the same day, suffered from the same ailments, and generally followed the same life pattern, but in ordinary human, rather than royal, terms.

Jung was born with the Sun placed in the fire sign of Leo. This makes a statement about the essential character qualities of the man: an independent spirit, a high degree of intuitive perception, a concern with the imaginative or spiritual dimensions of life, and a dislike of any authority other than his own voice. Given that he focused his efforts on understanding and healing collective as well as individual suffering, he would, being a typical fire sign temperament, do this in highly individualistic, sometimes provocative, and always original ways. An aura of the dramatic and the larger-than-life often clings to fire sign people, and Jung was no exception.

Of all the Western philosophers of this century, C.G.Jung provides the most accessible and beautiful form of understanding of religiousness and its relationship to human society.

On the following pages, we take a close look at Jung's astrological natal chart and the ways his character influenced his genius to project onto the world.

Jung and Osho had much in common, one from the East and one from the West, but both bringing a similar message and possessing very similar astrological traits.

Jung's ideas brought to the Western mind the concept of a global consciousness, a synergy between all things that could influence the individual throughout life. This version of Eastern understanding bathed Western intelligence with a fresh shower of ideas, and forms the very basis for the future.

Jung had the sun placed at the Descendant in his birth chart. This means that he found his sense of meaning in life through working for the welfare of others. The Descendant of 7th house cusp symbolizes one's interaction with others, and many people involved with teaching and healing have this placement. Freud also had it. On a deeper level, the Sun in the 7th house means that one's individual creative efforts may have a powerful effect on others. There may also be the need to found some kind of school, group, or organization to carry the "message" or ideas to a larger audience. The 7th house is a rather public house, and people with the Sun placed here do not tend to hide their light under the proverbial bushel.

Jung although born with the Sun in a fire sign, also had many planets in the element of Earth. This is a highly creative although tense combination, since Earth is the element of concrete reality. Jung's Moon was placed in an earth sign so that on the emotional level and in his personal life he was far more realistic and grounded, and also perhaps more withdrawn and self-contained than he appeared to be to those involved in his work. Also, he was shrewd in terms of financial and business dealing. Unlike many individuals involved in esoteric ideas, he could handle money extremely intelligently and could also ground his ideas in practical working methods and techniques. In other words, he was a practical idealist – a good pointer for the future of religion – who saw a lot more than he said and knew perfectly well that much of his vision could not be translated without subsequent distortion. Jung possessed a great distaste for "followers," although he loved a good audience. It is noticeable also that the Moon in an Earth sign tends to give a very basic and earthy sense of humor, that was clearly present in Jung's personality.

Jung had an air sign on the ascendant – Aquarius. This reflects a gift of articulateness and a capacity to communicate the sometimes very diffuse vision of the fire sign Sun. An air sign on the ascendant is also a socially adept creature – and Jung had the ability to charm (as did Osho,

C.G. JUNG

Date: July 26 1875 ❖ Time: 19:32 ❖ Place: Basel, Switzerland
Long: 7e35' ❖ Lat: 47n33' ❖ GMT: 19:02:16 ❖ Sidereal Time: 15:48:51

the "man of ornate speeches"), to sway audiences, to find the right way to phrase things. He also expressed a capacity to order his thinking and to formulate ideas in a coherent and clear fashion.

Jung had Aquarius on the ascendant, so would have been sensitive to the new idea now forming in the collective psyche. Although it is not possible to be intimate to the ideas of so complex a man as Jung, it would seem that he had a distaste for externalizing God and projecting a quasi-human "parent figure" into the heavens. He also seemed to recognize the close proximity, if not identity, of what was "dark" or hidden in human nature with what contains the seeds of the divine – he did not split body and spirit, but saw the human being as a whole. The curious mix of spirituality and psychology in his character seems to confuse many people who need to preserve this split. He also did not separate a spiritual life from the need to get one's act together on the Earth plane through hard work. This reflects the fire/earth blend in his chart. Discipline and structure were important to Jung, who despised laziness and felt that many "ailments" arose from a simple refusal to deal with reality – one's own and that of the world. He also gave great value to the healing power of the imagination, and the tremendous force of images and fantasy though music, painting, and poetry, as well as through psychology or meditative work.

It is hoped that from this description of two major characters in our recent past it will become clearer to the reader what might be the direction of our future religious understanding, and the birth of something new within the world of the divine. The main essence of this, both according to Nostradamus' choice of Osho as an example, and hopefully our astrological character study of Jung, is the presence of god within the individual, or rather the presence of holiness or religiousness within us all without the need to rely on some outside figure who dictates that life is ESSENTIALLY suffering and that heaven comes only after death. In the new world of god, paradise is in the here and now.

Chapter 6

MOTHER EARTH & THE GLOBAL SHIFT

MONG THE QUATRAINS OF *The Centuries* there are many that seem to point toward change and disruption in our climate and the ways in which Mother Earth responds to our human presence. They range from the bizarre, such as "rains of milk," to straight-forward predictions of earthquakes, volcanic eruptions, and massive tidal waves. There is even a quatrain that has been interpreted to predict a shift in the planet's axis.

Nostradamus was also very keen on science and medicine, naturally enough, as he was not primarily a prophet but a doctor.

So in the first part of this chapter we will take a look at some of the dramatic and powerful events that we might expect to occur through our environment.

Above ~ One of the huge "island" icebergs breaking off from the southern iceflows. The axis shift of the earth which is predicted to occur in the year 2005 would have massive repercussions as the oceans would find new levels and the lands new climate zones.

Opposite ~ Mount Etna overflowed on April 15, 1992 near the Italian village of Zafferana.

Nostradamus gave us many instances of natural disaster in our future. Every aspect of catastrophe is proposed including volcanoes, earthquakes, floods and even rains of milk.

Aprés la pluie lait assez longuette,
En plusieurs lieux de Reims le ciel touché:
Hélas quel meurtre de sang prés d'eux s'aprête,
Péres et fils Rois n'oseront approcher.
C3 18

"After the long rain of milk, in several places in Reims the sky touched: Alas, what a bloody murder is prepared near them, fathers and sons Kings will not dare approach."

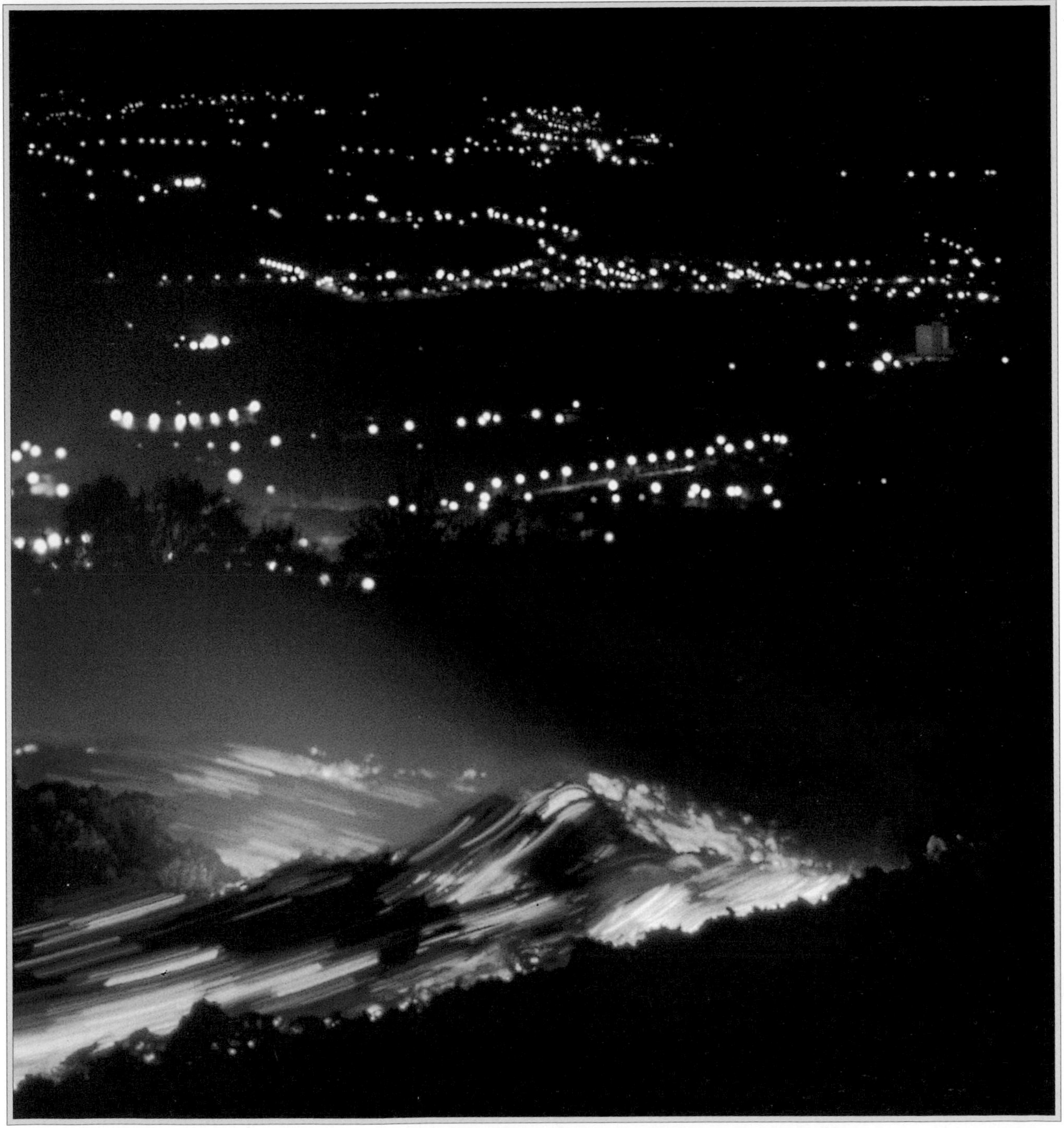

The Unquiet Sky

THROUGHOUT MANKIND'S HISTORY there have been many instances of phenomena involving the falling of the most unlikely items from the sky. In the Bible there are numerous instances of raining stones, frogs, fish, and grain. And in the recent past reports are equally numerous. In Dublin, Ireland, on May 9, 1867 a policeman had to take shelter from an onslaught of berries and nuts that fell from the sky "in great quantities and with great force" during "a tremendous rainfall." When picked up, the berries were said to be in "the form of a very small orange, about half an inch in diameter, black in color, and, when cut across, seem as if made of some hard dark brown wood. They also possess a slight aromatic odor."

Fire was seen to fall from the sky like for about 10 minutes on the night of October 18, 1867 at Thames Ditton in England. In the morning, water troughs and puddles were thickly covered with a deposit of sulphur.

On August 1, 1869 flesh and blood fell from the sky for three minutes and covered some two acres of land near Los Nietos in California, the flesh falling in thin strips about six inches long. Short, fine hairs also fell with it.

So Nostradamus' claim that milk and blood will fall as rain is not necessarily so obscure. The most likely direct association with this prophecy is that of a falling of acid rain, however, though there have been some suggestions that the quatrain concerning "blood and milk" (C3 19) might have something to do with semen and blood in relation to AIDS. The quatrain outlines the possibility of an instance of climate extremes occurring in the Mediterranean in both cases. The verse above refers to Reims, and quatrain C3 19 mentions Lucca, a small town near the coast of Italy.

In 1992 one of the most devastating hurricanes (Andrew) swept up the coast of the US and caused enormous harm to areas of Florida, destroying homes and killing many people. The meteorological investigators, following this climatic attack, surmised that due to the increase in the warming of the Earth, such extremes of weather could be more common in the future. Given a powerful volcanic eruption combined with a tornado or hurricane off the Mediterranean, raining milk (acid rain) and even raining blood would seem a likely result.

Hurricane "David" struck Martinique in 1979, causing massive damage and loss of life in the region. Yet still in the years to come, mankind apparently will not successfully predict the weather.

Above ~ *A bird dies in an oil spill off the coast of Saudi Arabia.*

Of all the animals and creatures on planet Earth, mankind has done the greatest damage to natural life. His capacity for destruction seems almost endless. New methods of killing animals and plant and tree life are invented every year. In the 1990s we are in the era of the massive oil spill. Every time we say that something must be done, and soon there is another spill. The way of the near future, after 1996, will be the way of the ozone holes, and this time it will not only be animal life that is destroyed but human life too.

1996 ~ SECRET FIRES & THE FOOD CHAIN

L'an que Saturne et Mars égaux combust,
L'air fort séché longue trajection:
Par feux secrets d'ardeur grand lieu adust,
Peu pluie, vent chaud, guerres, incursions.
C4 67

"The year that Saturn and Mars are equally burning, the air is very dry with a long shooting star (or meteor): through secret fires a great place blazes burned by the sun, little rain, warm wind, wars, incursions."

THIS IS OUR FRIEND NOSTRADAMUS at his most dramatic and poetic. "The year that Saturn and Mars are equally burning" is, of course, an astrological reference and involves a conjunction that is not uncommon. The next most likely date for this is when they are together in Pisces, and Mercury is conjunct Mars on March 22, 1996. It is not difficult even for the most untried interpreter to make sense of the rest of the verse. We are told that, at that time, the air will become extremely dry and that a great place will be set fire through the heat of the Sun. At the same time there will be very little rain, warm winds, and a shooting star or meteor that will pass by on a long trajectory.

The whole scenario fits exactly with the results already felt in the early 1990s, where the ozone holes have increased the effects of the Sun's heat on the planet's surface. Forest fires are more regular, and it would seem likely that the "great place" that is burned by the Sun's heat in 1996 could be another large forest that burns out of control. The fact that the fire is said to be "secret" may be hinting that it is begun without the initial knowledge of any fire control teams.

The depletion of larger areas of the ozone in our atmosphere in the future would fulfill this prediction. In the early 1990s there are already holes over Europe, Scandinavia, Australia, and North America, as well as the first hole that appeared over the South Pole. The story continues with another verse that takes us further down the avenue of ecological problems.

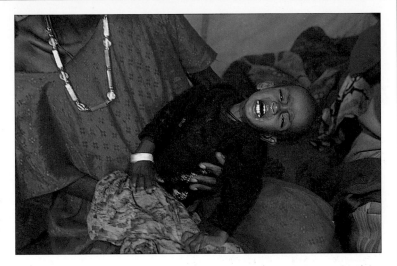

Si grande famine par onde pestifre,
Par pluie longue le long du pôle arctique:
Samarobryn cent lieues de l'hemisphére,
Vivront sans loi exempt de politique.
C6 5

"A very great famine through pestilent wave, through long rain the length of the arctic pole: Samarobryn one hundred leagues from the hemisphere, they will live without law exempt from politics."

One of the most recent scientific projections that has arisen out of the new conditions set by ozone holes is that the food chain is ultimately affected by the excess ultraviolet waves received on the Earth's surface. The larger the holes get, the greater the climatic response and in turn the greater the impact on animal life.

Cattle and sheep in Australia, New Zealand, and South America are apparently suffering from cataracts caused by ultraviolet rays leaking through the atmosphere. In turn, the increasing temperature caused by the greenhouse effect changes climatic patterns and ultimately the whole ecology of the land itself. Mass starvation in Africa has been the first impact, but we will see more of this in the future if the problem is not resolved.

The reference, "Samarobryn one hundred leagues from the hemisphere, they will live without law exempt from politics," is intended to guide us toward the times when these climatic changes affect our situation most severely. "Samarobryn" or "Samarobriva" was the ancient, pre-Roman name given to the French city of Amiens, now capital of the Somme department in the region of Picardie. The city is north of Paris and was well known in Nostradamus' time as a textile-producing area of France.

Evidently, during the time when the world feels the greatest impact of "A very great famine through pestilent wave, through long rain the length of the arctic pole..." Amiens will be involved in a political turmoil.

Above ~ The Kabre Bayah refugee camp in Ethiopia houses thousands of sick and dying children. Nostradamus would have viewed scenes such as this one as part of our present and future. It is no wonder he saw us full of doom and disaster.

Earth Shaking

Earthquakes abound in our future. California is, of course, the favorite for the worst quakes, but Nostradamus directs us to many other instances when the Earth and the people on it will shake beyond control.

Le tremblement de terre à Mortara,
Cassich saint George à demi perfondrez,
Paix assoupie, la guerre esveillera,
Dans temple à Pasques abismes enfondrez.
C9 31

"The earthquake at Mortara, Cassich saint George half sunk, numbed by peace, war arises, in the temple at Easter the ground opens up."

THIS QUATRAIN HAS BEEN COMMONLY INTERPRETED to refer to the sinking of the lower part of England into the sea, connected in some way with an earthquake in Italy. This idea has been given additional strength by a prediction from Edgar Cayce that echoes the prophecy and dates the event in the year 2000. Mortara is in Italy, 1,000 miles from England, so the earthquake that is predicted to happen would not be the source of flooding in southern England. The word "Cassich" cannot be found anywhere. But some interpretors have attributed it, for lack of any other meaning, to the Greek word "Cassiterides," the name given to Cornwall and the Scilly Isles in the south of England, a district also known as the "tin islands." The translation and interpretation therefore, in popular form, has been: "The trembling of the Earth at Mortara the tin island of St. George half sunk..." We tend to accept the most popular forms of interpretations of Nostradamus as though they were true, and forevermore England is due to sink into the sea! It is as if we would like that to happen and therefore believe in the prediction. Whereas there is another alternative, particularly because earthquakes in that region of the world are rare.

The island of St. George is one of the oldest English settlements in the Western Hemisphere and still exists under the same name in northern Bermuda. It is a tiny island and much more likely to be affected by earthquake activity than England's south coast. The reference to "Cassich" remains obscure, but if the popular interpretation is correct there may be some connection between the "tin islands" of southern England and the fact that St. George's Island became British just 50 years after Nostradamus' death.

Another earthquake prediction gives us a precise time:

> *"Sun twenty degrees of Taurus the earth will tremble strongly, the great filled theater will ruin: the air, sky obscured and troubled, then the infidel will call upon God and the saints."*

Interpreters have assumed much from this verse. For example, the mention of "theater" in the lines has led them to believe that the region for this quake will be California because of the presence of Hollywood.

Nostradamus believed that earthquakes and other natural disasters were a retribution for ungodliness, and that as mankind moved further from his religion so the disaster would increase.

But the world tries to help, bringing aid to Ethiopia – at least a start.

The Sun passes through twenty degrees of Taurus every year on April 10th, and, coincidentally, there was a massive eruption of Mt. Etna in the spring of 1992, causing fears that the nearby village of Taormina with its celebrated Greek amphitheater would be destroyed. So, we may have seen this prophecy already fulfilled, though the amphitheater at Taormina was not "ruined."

In another verse, we find a suspiciously close rendering of the hurricane that swept through Florida in 1992:

> *"The great city of the maritime Ocean, surrounded by a crystal swamp, in the winter solstice and the spring, will be tried by terrible wind." (C9 48)*

In century 6, verse 88, we hear:
> *"A great kingdom will remain desolate, near the Ebro they will be gathered in assemblies. The Pyrenees mountains will console him (or it), when in May lands will tremble."*

In this case we have the beginning of another common theme throughout the quatrains. Evidently, not only will the earthquakes disrupt the world continually, but whole areas of civilized cities and towns will be left desolate as the occupants move away from them. In this case, the location is the Ebro river in Northern Spain.

In another verse:

> *"The new empire in desolation, it will be changed by the northern pole, from Sicily will come the disturbance, to trouble the enterprise tributary to Philip."*

Perhaps the troubles in this case relate to the revolution in Italy that we examined in Chapter Four, though the name Philip has no relation to any significant individual in the 20th century yet.

Earth Shifting

A S A FINAL CRESCENDO TO THE potential disasters that Nostradamus interpreters imagine for Mother Earth, surely the very zenith is the shifting of the planetary axis that is seen predicted within several quatrains to be most likely to take place at some time during the last years of the 1990s and into the 21st century. We are told about this through many examples, but here we will quote just two of them. First, from Nostradamus' epistle to his king, Henry II, which, as we have already seen, contained many astonishing predictions.

"There will be omens in the spring, and extraordinary changes thereafter, reversals of nations and mighty earthquakes. And there shall be in the month of October a great movement of the Globe, and it will be such that one will think the Earth has lost it natural gravitational movement and that it will be plunged into the abyss of perpetual darkness." *Epistle to Henry II.*

And second, one of the many verses that touches upon the likely results of such a shift.

"Earth-shaking fire from the center of the Earth will cause trembling around the new city. Two great rocks will make war for a long time. Then Arethusa will redden in a new river." (C1 87)

Given our natural fears of everything, and our human expectation of disaster, together with the end of millennium scenario that everything is going to vanish into the abyss anyway, these two predictions would seem valid enough as confirmations that everything we ever expected that was bad, was also right. Here there is "earth-shaking fire" and "trembling around the new city," plus "two great rocks warring against each other"

The scenario of the global axis shift is already quite familiar. The polar ice caps will melt because of global warming and the oceans will rise. Because of a change in the balance of water and earth, so the rotating globe will slip slightly and spin off its normal axis.

The result, of course, would be a repeat of the destruction of the dinosaurs millions of years ago, and human beings would be the ones to suffer. This is our greatest fear.

But probably the truth is less dramatic, and has more to do with the internal changes that mankind will undergo around the end of the millennium. There are many astrological indications for a major change in gestalt as planets line up in unusual alignments, coinciding with auguries from the past. There is no doubt that the end of the "second millennium" will be a highly dramatic moment in human history.

– clearly indicating the rubbing of the plates beneath the ground that leads to massive earthquakes. Then there is "a great movement of the globe," clearly, in our apocalyptic minds, a shift in the Earth's planetary axis – certain death for everyone, and we will end our days as did the dinosaurs. And it's not as though it isn't possible. With the melting of the polar icecap there is the likelihood that the Earth will become "top-heavy" and shift in from its normal spin. What a way to go.

But maybe this is not all that is going to happen. Maybe all this is simply the physical manifestation of something which will strongly effect us in a different way also.

First, we know that there will always be earthquakes. And in the same way as Nostradamus had a tendency to see our wars in the 20th century as the holocaust, so also he must have seen the earthquakes as massive and earth shattering – that they are. But this "great movement of the globe" – is it really referring to just a physical shift, or could it also be a massive shift of consciousness, a change in Earth's gestalt?

We have seen in several parts of this book that there does appear to be, on the horizon, a major new paradigm that will touch almost everyone on the planet. We can expect a new religiousness that will transform thousands of years of belief systems, and bring us perhaps closer to a personal understanding of God. We can see also, that in political, economic, social, and national boundaries, the borderlines are going to shift dramatically over the last years of the 20th century and the first years of the 21st century. It appears clearly that Nostradamus did see a global shift, but perhaps he was also describing the people and their relationship with Mother Earth.

Chapter 7
MATTERS OF THE HEART

Nostradamus saw that everything would change in the 21st century. He saw that men and women would take on new roles and that women especially would become more powerful than ever before. We have to admit, it's about time for this.

AMONG NOSTRADAMUS' VERSES there are many that appear to make no sense at all. Commentators in the past have tended to attribute these either to the future – believing that each generation picks up the meaning of more and still more of them as events catch up – or to the meanderings of a man who was part magician and part madman. In any event a lot of intuition and imagination is needed to look forward through the verses because, of course, one does not know what is coming. One can ultimately only suppose. Looking at the verses in this intuitive manner, it becomes interesting to note that some of them apply to areas of life other than the major themes of national or global change. In fact, some of them clearly do apply to more personal things, matters of the heart, we could say. The following is a sample of these, starting with a movement that has been long awaited, had tremendous build-up, and that has hopefully a wonderful future.

"The moon hidden in deep shadows, her brother passes by rusty colored: the great one masked for a long time beneath eclipses, iron will cool in the bloody wound."

The Shadowed Moon

HE WOMEN'S MOVEMENT, feminism, egalitarianism, equality of the sexes, whatever we wish to call it, began to flourish during this century. Until its birth, women had a bad deal, largely at the hands of men and the society men created. The situation has changed dramatically since the two world wars, and it will rise still further to prominence. Nostradamus describes this progress with the utmost clarity, care, and understanding. His wisdom is quite breathtaking, even on the surface of these lines.

The Moon has been hidden in deep shadows for many centuries. During his time, women were intended for marriage and childrearing. We do not even know the name of Nostradamus' first wife; for those who recorded such things a woman's name was of little importance against the superiority of the man.

The woman, even today, in many parts of the world, is expected to behave in a fixed manner, mostly at home with the kids. The difficulties that she faces when attempting to rise, for example, within the business world are far greater than those a man has to undergo in a world where club members, drinking buddies, and boards of directors are still predominantly male. But all that will change. "...Her brother passes by rusty colored." This comment was written with a touch of wry humor, that men will go rusty as their power deteriorates and women grow stronger in matters of the world's development. "...The great one masked for a long time beneath eclipses." Nostradamus' poetry continues to use the metaphor of the Moon all through the verse, here expressing the state of feminine power beneath the eclipses of the Moon.

And finally, the most powerful line in the verse, "...iron will cool in the bloody wound." The power created and encouraged by men, that of the weapon (iron), will be cooled in the bloody wound of womanhood (menstruation). One could not find a more appropriate description of the change in the balance of the sexes likely to occur during the 21st century. It may be that the whole progress that Nostradamus sees humanity making, as outlined in previous chapters, from chaos and corruption to a new golden age, is brought about through that one simple line: "Tidira fer dans la plaie sanguine."

Humans take a very long time to make major changes. We will see the 100 year anniversary of the women's movement around 2012 - a century after the Suffragettes began their campaign for equality, and the job will not be done even then.

The Royals & The Family

Le Royal sceptre sera contraint de prendre, .
Ce que ses predecesseurs avoient engaige:
Puis que l'aneau on fera mal entendre,
Lors qu'on viendra le palais saccager.
C7 23

"The Royal sceptre will have to accept that which his predecessors
have employed. Because they do not understand the ring when they
come to destroy the palace."

NE OF THE MOST FUNDAMENTAL ASPECTS of society that will undergo changes in the last years of this millennium and the first of the next will be the family.

The first signs of "unrest" within the hallowed portals of family life were seen when the instance of divorce showed signs of increase shortly after World War I. By the 1960s and 1970s, one in three marriages were ending in divorce, and today the statistics don't make a lot of sense because many more couples are simply not bothering to get married at all.

The recent "scandals" surrounding the British royal family exemplify the often unsatisfactory processes of formal marriage. Nostradamus has chosen to use the example of Charles and Diana as part of his continuing story of the unfolding developments of 20th-century life.

It is true that we are seeing currently a resurgence of interest in family security. We only need to look at media advertising to see this trend, where there is a kind of "running for shelter" in every quarter. This is once again an example of the fear that is engendered by change.

The overall trend, apart from this terror of change, is a major new paradigm in the conditions of family life. Pluto continues to portray its characteristic pattern of bringing poisons to the surface, such as child

Royalty in England has taken a great deal of criticism, and has had to deal with a lot of incidental problems during the 1990s. Many of the difficulties have been related to family values, in particular marital values.

Nostradamus gave us a clear indicator to the future in the verse on the opposite page. This is one of those bizarre situations where the authors saw the predictions come to fruition during the writing of the book. From the completion of the main text to the time when the captions were written (about two months) Prince Charles and Princess Diana announced their intention to separate.

abuse, rape between partners, and other hidden tendencies, so that changes at a deeper level can be accomplished. And on the positive side we begin to see that there may be other ways of raising our children in the world – ways that are ultimately happier for both adults and children.

Aquarius is concerned primarily with friendship and partnership before sex and the body. The world of ideas is, for Aquarians, the essential reality. It is rather like Plato's concept that there are Divine Ideas of which the physical world is a reflection. The body is important to Aquarius, but as an idea rather than a sensuous reality. Sex is also important, but once again it is a realm of ideas, fantasy, communication, anticipation, concepts of "healthy" sex, and experimentation, that carries more value than the purely physical experience. The "forbidden" element of sex that was so prevalent during the Piscean Christian era is alien to Aquarius, for whom all things should be clear and understandable. Hence there is a gradually increasing volume of sex manuals, emphasis on sex education, and so on, that reflect an almost scientific or rational approach to the whole realm. So this characteristic affects the way in which we look upon relationships during the Aquarian Age.

Collective care for children will become of greater importance, including communal families where childcare is undertaken by the group rather than the birth parents. Architectural experiments will return the arrangement of homes into building designs that echo the Spanish *Corale* and Le Corbusier's "Radial City" in Marseilles, France built in the 1950s.

In the Aquarian Age partnership is based upon friendship, so sexual jealousy and the painful tensions that exist within sexual relationships will become of less importance. This is not to say that sexual relationships will not continue to exist, but they will not necessarily form a basis for marriage and childrearing. We will not imagine in the 21st century that we must necessarily go the route of education, marriage, mortgage, family, and security, because we will have seen the result of that trend _ a result that is too often unhappy, as in the case of the British royal family, trapped within the bounds of "that which his predecessors have employed."

Communes (such as the kibbutz in Israel) will grow in importance as a system, among other things, for the rearing of children. The mother and father will be the prime role models for the birth-child, but there will be plenty of uncles, aunts, godfathers, and godmothers to take over when the birth-parents are unavailable or no longer together. The child will be able to turn to numerous loving and concerned adults to find support.

This will have the effect also of broadening the child's view of the world – so much confined in the 20th century to the anxieties of the four-walled family unit.

For Aquarians, blood ties – family – are not as important as "like minds." The family, to Aquarius, is the human family, and a friendship may mean more than the fact that somebody happens to be an uncle or cousin or even a parent or child. Aquarians are sometimes accused of coldness in their personal relationships, but they are not cold – simply more orientated toward affinity of mind and spirit than toward more concrete bonds.

Many aspects of the changes we are already undergoing will lead to this result.

Nostradamus sees the process through various verses, one of which gives us the impression that Britain's Prince Charles may get caught up in the transformation of marriage and family and thereby may be the last sovereign ruler of England.

"Because they do not understand the ring when they come to destroy the palace."

Another verse tends to confirm this story:

If Charles is permitted to reach the throne, it appears that his reign will be short and his position will be taken by the next heir to the British Throne, his son.
But all this has a powerful effect on the whole attitude of the people in relation to marriage and family. Further changes in this area of life may be expected by the end of the millennium.

Pour ne vouloir consentir au divorce,
Qui puis aprés sera connu indigne:
Le Roi des Iles sera chassé par force,
Mis à son lieu qui de roi n'aura signe.
C10 22

"For not wishing to consent to the divorce, that then afterwards will be recognized as unworthy: the King of the Isles will be driven out by force, in his place put one who will have no mark of a king."

This verse does not fit well within any other reign of the English throne. The closest possibilities are Charles I, II, James II, and Edward VIII (later the Duke of Windsor), who abdicated in favor of his American wife. Yet none of the first three actually divorced, and Edward VIII does not fit the verse in other ways.

Poor Charles III, it seems from these lines, is to be our next most likely candidate to fulfill this rather distressing prediction. Though if we

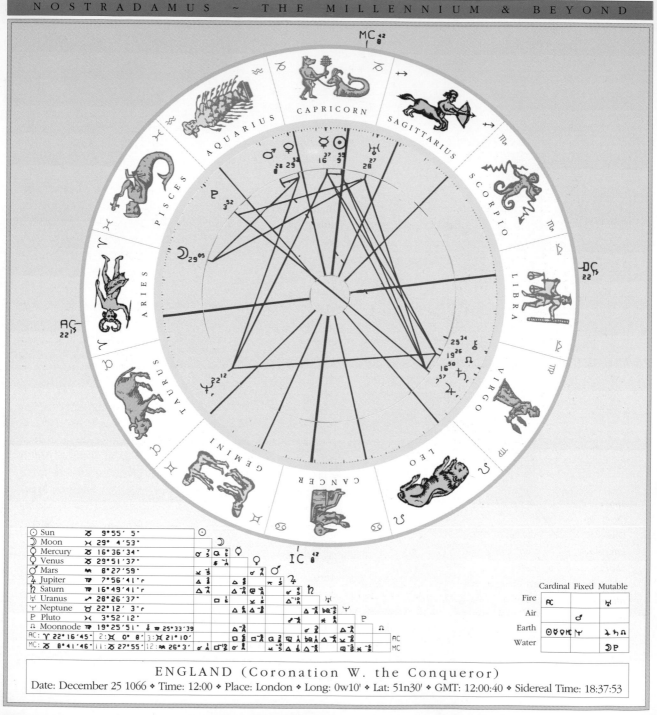

☉ Sun	♐ 9°55′ 5″			
☽ Moon	♓ 29° 4′53″			
☿ Mercury	♐ 16°36′34″			
♀ Venus	♐ 29°51′37″			
♂ Mars	♏ 8°27′59″			
♃ Jupiter	♍ 7°56′41″ r			
♄ Saturn	♍ 16°49′41″ r			
♅ Uranus	♐ 28°26′37″			
♆ Neptune	♉ 22°12′ 3″ r			
♇ Pluto	♓ 3°52′12″			
☊ Moonnode	♍ 19°25′51″			
AC: ♈ 22°16′45″	2:♉ 0° 8″	3:♓ 21°10″		
MC: ♉ 8°41′46″	11:♉ 27°55″	12:♈ 26°3″		

	Cardinal	Fixed	Mutable
Fire	AC		♅
Air		♂	
Earth	☉☿♀♅♈		♃♄☊
Water			☽♇

ENGLAND (Coronation W. the Conqueror)
Date: December 25 1066 ✦ Time: 12:00 ✦ Place: London ✦ Long: 0w10′ ✦ Lat: 51n30′ ✦ GMT: 12:00:40 ✦ Sidereal Time: 18:37:53

Above ~ *A 13th century portrait of William the Conqueror.*

One of the special problems that England has, in regard to marital and family changes, is its long tradition of Victorianism, which tends to cause a rather repressed attitude to sexual relationships, especially when they don't work.

look at the astrological indications for this future period, the indications are not quite so drastic.

The chart for England, based on the crowning of William the Conqueror in 1066, has the Sun in nine degrees Capricorn, and is not being affected by the heavy planets until 2012, when Pluto transiting through Capricorn reaches the British Sun. There is another British chart based on the founding of the United Kingdom, that also has the Sun in Capricorn, at 10 degrees, virtually the same place as the original 1066 chart. So, whichever chart we refer to, Pluto arrives at this point in 2012.

Looking at various countries that have been affected by Pluto transits across their natal Sun positions reflects major changes in their essential way of governing. On the other hand, the birth chart for the EEC (born January 1, 1958) also has the Sun in 10 degrees Capricorn, and America's Sun in 13 Cancer is not far away. So this reflects not so much an abdication by Charles, or the end of the British monarchy, but a more global government involving many Western countries, leaving their constitutional monarchs alone but affecting the structure of central government.

In any event the society that runs for shelter against inevitable change will need to find scapegoats for its conservative attitudes. The British royal family is a perfect candidate for this narrowmindedness and the media have already demonstrated their deeply traditional attitudes in the way in which they probed and tortured Charles and Diana during 1992. Once Charles reaches the throne itself, the problems he may be having as a member of a new generation forced into old values, will not stop. Then, however, he will be king, and as such expected to behave in an even more traditional manner. This is likely to herald major difficulties for him and, with some move towards a more global government, his position will be changed – at least in relation to what it has been until now. It will also herald a change in basic family values, including those that have caused the British to be sexually repressed.

We can see this story unfold in two other quatrains, one of which gives us a broad picture.

UNITED KINGDOM
Date: January 1 1801 ❖ Time: 0:00
Place: London
Long: 0w10' ❖ Lat: 51n30' ❖ GMT: 0:00
Sidereal Time: 6:39:59

According to the two natal charts that are relevant to England, the effect of transiting Pluto, our faithful "house-cleaner" and detoxifier, will not be greatly felt until 2012. However, difficulties related to government, the royalty family and in particular Prince Charles, will hit the country for some time yet. It is not that Charles will actually have to abdicate his throne in the near future, but that the royal family of England will be affected by powerful changes in world government matters.

Le changement sera fort difficile:
Cite, province au change gain fera:
Coeur haut, prudent mis, chasse lui habile,
Mer, terre, peuple son etat changera.
C4 21

"The change will be very difficult: city, province will gain by the change: Heart high, prudence given, chased out by skill, sea, land, people will change their state."

Amongst the 965 verses in *The Centuries* there are a number like this – rather vague and without any real hint of time or geographical reference. The most significant factor, however, is that as we become familiar with these verses, what we might call "atmospheric" verses, it becomes evident that Nostradamus peppered his work with them deliberately, wishing to provide general hints as to changes in mankind's nature.

The most prominent words in this verse are "Heart high, prudence given..." Nostradamus points once again to a period of our evolution in which there are difficulties in adjusting to change, and yet the heart is at the forefront of life, and the changes are generally seen to be good for humanity. We could hardly say that of the last part of the 20th century. But we might find it applicable to the first part of the 21st century.

The other quatrain that is relevant to this subject brings us a more convoluted and descriptive version of the same story of change in marriage and family.

Quand l'adultere blesse sans coup aura
Meurtri la femme et la fils par depit:
Femme assommee l'enfant etranglera:
Huit captifs pris, s'etouffer sans repit.
C8 63

"When the adulterer wounded without a blow will have murdered his wife and the son through frustration: woman (wife) knocked out he will strangle the child: Eight captives taken, to suffocate without respite."

The majority of interpreters would normally attempt to match such a quatrain to some series of events. However, it is more appropriate to see this as a kind of descriptive verse of a condition in humanity in the future, and one that fits with other stories that Nostradamus has told us and that is appropriate in astrological and social terms.

Marriage, as a holy state (or indeed as any state), has become suspect, caging human beings into conditions that derived their need many centuries ago. Humanity has moved on and this cage is no longer effective or needed.

The verse describes a classic extreme situation within a family unit that has essentially gone wrong. "When the adulterer wounded without a blow..." This is about someone that has been wounded in the heart. No blow has been struck. "...will have murdered his wife and the son through frustration..." Here again, having set the tone of the "wound without a blow," we have "murder," the kind of murder that can take place only within the family – emotional murder, where the wife and child are trapped by jealousy, anxiety, and dependence. "Woman (or wife) knocked out, he will strangle the child..." Here again, an exact scenario for the repressed family unit, and one that we see again and again in modern society, where the "nuclear unit," rather than providing security, provides claustrophobia. Therapists continue to attempt to save formalized relationships when perhaps it would be better to reconsider the system that put them there in the first place. In any event, if we we put these verses in the context of the changes that are happening in the growth of the Aquarian Age, we may expect some very exciting, though perhaps sometimes disturbing, transformation to occur within marriage and family during the next decade or so.

And in the last line of the verse he gives us a specific event that is intended as a pointer to the time when all this will become most relevant. "Eight captives taken, to suffocate without respite."

EUROPEAN ECONOMIC COMMUNITY
Date: May 1 1958 ❖ Time: 0:00
Place: Brussels, Belgium
Long: 4e20' ❖ Lat: 50n 50' ❖ GMT: 23:00
Sidereal Time: 13:50:50

It seems as though Charles will be the King of England during the time when a first world power will be set up.

We have already discussed this in another part of the book, as Nostradamus tells us to expect the European Community, the United Nations and the United States to increase their supervision of world events during the 21st century.

The Heart of the Lover

Coeur de l'amant ouvert d'amour furtive
Dans le ruisseau fera ravir la Dame:
Le demi mal contrefera lascive,
Le pére à deux privera corps de l'âme.
C8 25

"The lover's heart is opened by furtive love the woman ravished by streams (of tears), the lascivious will mimic half a hurt, the father will twice do without the soul."

S WE HAVE SEEN SEVERAL TIMES BEFORE, the poetry of Nostradamus' expression, mixed with a kind of coded "discretion," produces something in translation that makes the head spin. But even at a first glance, if we listen a little to our more instinctive voice, we glean a sense from the lines. Here, the prophet speaks of changes in our attitudes toward love and sex.

Sexuality is a burning issue in every era of society, and during the 20th century it has undergone greater transformation that perhaps in any other previous age. With the advent of feminism and a far greater degree of power to the feminine spirit, we have seen an adjustment that is being felt across all realms of life: in psychiatry, medicine, crime, family, even disease and childbirth. It has become clear that our sexual well being is of paramount importance and is not something that can simply be swept beneath the carpet as a necessary evil or something pure required to bring the next generation into being. Happy sexual relationships, both with ourselves and with others, are part of our basic physical health, and many taboos have been banished with this knowledge.

In Nostradamus' time, self-awareness was not an integral part of life. The Piscean Age, as we have already discussed, was one where the

During this century sexual values have undergone a radical change. For the first time in literally thousands of years, there is a renewal of interest in the Goddess and her ways challenging the male domination of the last few millenia.
Above *~ the Venus of Lespugue from 25,000 years BCE symbolizing the Goddess as creatrix predating the male creator.*
Opposite *~ the Minoan Snake Goddess of Knossos in Greece (1800 BCE), symbol of sensuality and fertility.*

probing of individuality took little space in daily life, but since the advent of the Aquarian Age there seems to be little else to consider but the internal processes of self discovery.

In this verse, Nostradamus is as specific as a 16th century Renaissance man can be, considering the conditioning of his age. The first line simply outlines the state of the "art."

"The lover's heart is opened by furtive love..."

The way of the past has been that love (sex) has too often been engendered only through a rather repressed and essentially "pornographic" (in the widest sense) view of sexuality. Our approach to sexuality has derived from uncertainty and deeply ingrained conditioning. Parents still tend to avoid direct explanation of sexual behavior because they don't understand it well enough to be open and free with themselves, so they give the same format to their children. Sex education in schools still carries that element of guilt that makes children grow up with confusion. One of the most recent understandings within psychoanalysis, psychiatry, and sexual therapy is that young children, through adverse conditions of schooling and parenting, travel through from the love of the mother into the lust of society far too quickly by the "education" of the wrong people in the wrong circumstances. Single sex boarding schools (particularly in England) are probably the worst exponents (often unconsciously) of this process, insofar as young people, and particularly boys, have a way of educating one another in areas of sexuality that can sometimes prove to be disastrous in later life. Sex is very often "furtive," pornographic, and essentially unnatural, and it may take much of the rest of adulthood (if ever) for the man to recognize the reasons for his unhappy sexuality and unlearn them so that at least some part of his life can flow more freely and happily in relationships. And because sexuality is so intimately connected with the emotions, the result is a deeply disturbed individual who cannot express himself (or herself) at all. This in turn affects work, play, and of course, future generations as well.

Nostradamus goes on in the same line to give an example of how this sexual repression affects others, particularly women. "... The woman ravished by streams (of tears)..." The French word "ruisseau," if literally translated, means brook or stream. But if we add the words "de larmes," we have "floods of tears." Nostradamus often shortened his lines for poetic effect, leaving the interpretation to us. In this case he refers to the way women have had to suffer at the hands of the repressed, essentially male, social attitude to sexual freedom, and the result, as we know, has been much unhappiness.

"...the lascivious will mimic half a hurt..."

Here we find a most subtle piece of writing, expressing perfectly the reaction of those who have formulated this puritan attitude to sex and love. The "lascivious" are those who prefer to keep things the way they were, wishing to maintain suppression of attitudes in the belief that sex is something to be hidden, feigning "half a hurt" moral indignation.

The final line gives us the most enigmatic part of the verse: "...the father will twice do without the soul."

Fatherhood has long been one of the prime causes of difficulties both for fathers and children. As we have suggested in previous interpretations, there seems to be an indication within the astrological tendencies of the Aquarian Age toward greater emphasis on communal living, or at least a broadening of the family values away from the tightness of the nuclear family and into the concepts of friendship and shared resources. The "soul" of the father, under these circumstances, would emerge into a wider and more generous state. We could almost suggest that children might be loved and nourished by lots of "Uncles" (friends) rather than one father, and that the responsibility to provide for children's education in the broadest sense and in particular in terms of sexuality and love, might change, within the 21st century, into something happier through this maturity of vision.

As attitudes become more liberal and men more flexible, so the processes that men experience during their lives become more mature and advanced. Nostradamus saw even these soft and subtle changes in humanity, though whether men will ever actually give birth is not reflected in the prophet's verses.

Would you be more careful if it was you that got pregnant?

215

Chapter 8

FUN & PHENOMENA

N OSTRADAMUS, as we may now have gathered, was not only concerned with major events, massive wars, political disasters and gigantic earthquakes, although these events clearly occupied the greater part of his awareness of the future, as somehow they rise above the current of activities on this planet.

He concerned himself also with a lighter, more individualistic side of humanity, and this chapter will take a brief look at just two examples of this side of the prophet's interest in our world. We finish on this note, to balance the often overpowering nature of the prophet's predictions for our future.

We start with a magnificent and highly documented treasure hunt.

"The images bloated by gold and silver, that after the rape were thrown into the fire, at the discovery all dulled and troubled, on the marble inscriptions, prescripts inserted.

At the fourth pillar where they dedicate to Saturn, split by earthquake and flood: under the Saturnin edifice an urn found, of gold carried off by Caepio and then restored.

Within Toulouse not far from Beluzer, digging a deep pit, palace of spectacle: the treasure found will come to vex everyone, and all in two places and near the Basacle."

Les simulacres d'or et d'argent enfles,
Qu'apres le rapt au feu furent jetes,
Au decouvert etients tous et troubles,
Au marbre ecrits, prescits interjetes.

Au quart pilier l'on sacre a Saturne,
Par tremblant terre et deluge fendu:
Sous l'edifice Saturnin trouvee urne,
D'or Capion ravi et puis rendu.

Dedans Tholouse non loin de Beluzer,
Faisant un puits loins, palais de spectacle:
Tresor trouve un chacun ira vexer,
Et en deux locs tout et pres delvasacle.
C8 28, 29, 30

Heaven is out, the individual spirit and a resident godliness is in during the last few years of the 20th century.
By the 21st century god will mean something completely different.
Above *~ The Delphic oracle at Toulouse where Nostradamus tells us there is a vast treasure of gold buried and yet to be found – until treasure hunters in the last years of the 1990s take their diggers and follow the map given by the prophet.*

The Treasure Hunt

HIS IS ACKNOWLEDGED BY most interpreters to be one of the most interesting combinations of verses in all of the quatrains. To understand the treasure hunt provided, we first need to look at the historical and legendary background – the source of this treasure.

In the 4th and 3rd centuries before Christ, the Gauls (French) went to war in a fairly catastrophic fashion. First they sacked Rome in 390 BCE. Rome was the cultural empire of the Western world. Then in 279 BCE they invaded Greece and continued on to Asia. They battled and generally raped this part of the world for almost half a century and then settled down in a place called Galatia. The people of Toulouse, however, have a slightly different viewpoint, in that they believe through their own legends that it was the "Volcae-Tectosages" of Toulouse who performed this incredible world-shattering act of war, returning to their own country with the spoils and treasures from the two heads of the classical world that resulted from their efforts.

Included in the local legend (though not in the historical records), their plunder included severe damage to the Oracle of Apollo at Delphi, one of the world's most treasured and hallowed centers of power. When they returned, a terrible plague broke out in the area of Toulouse in retribution for this ghastly act of sacrilege, as confirmed by their local Oracle, who acted like a kind of sub-office of the head office in Delphi, or so the legend goes.

The local Oracle informed them that the plague would continue until they took all the treasures they had plundered and cast them into a sacred lake, the location of which we are not given by the legend. Some recent scholars believe that this sacred lake may simply have been a hole in the ground, though no one has established the truth until now.

According to historical records the town of Toulouse was very rich in gold. This may have been simply because local mining in the Pyrenees enriched the area, but it may also be because some of the stolen treasure was not actually buried in the sacred lake. No one knows – yet.

"The Demon of the Plague" - This engraving from 1540 was a visual representation of the terrible visitations of the disease, flying above the heads of potential victims. Toulouse was visited by just such retribution because of its involvement in the theft of Delphic gold.

When the Germanic tribes called the Cimbri invaded Gaul, the Volcae-Tectosages broke their alliance with Rome and moved to the side of the invaders. The Roman Consul, Caepio, who had been sent to fight the Cimbri, used this as an opportunity to plunder Toulouse in 106 BCE. The Cimbri managed to completely destroy the Roman army under Caepio in what amounted to Rome's most serious defeat ever, and the plundered gold taken from Toulouse never reached Rome.

The legend to which Nostradamus refers holds that the stolen treasure was buried beneath the church of Saint Saturnin-du-Taur ("...under the Saturnin edifice an urn found..."), that had been built on a "sacred lake." It is also presumed within historical reference books of the area (*Histoire de Toulouse* – Cayla & Paviot) that the treasure is still buried beneath this church.

Nostradamus is telling us that the treasure will be found. Perhaps it will be found by some enterprising reader of his quatrains.

Line one of the second verse seems to tell us precisely where the first clue will be found, while line four shows us just how Nostradamus managed to mix the historical story with the local legend. This is not to say that we necessarily know better than him. He was, after all, nearer to it than we are.

The name "Bazacle" is common in Toulouse as the name of a local castle and a local area within the town that was associated with milling.

Within the three verses there are two good reasons why the treasure will be found. First, Nostradamus tells us that it will be due to volcanic eruptions, and then later that workmen digging the ground will find the treasure. Line three of verse three also suggests that there is a natural discovery. Perhaps all three will be the answer. The distance between the Bazacle castle and the church of Saint Saturnin is about half a mile. The treasure could be buried somewhere in that area.

Of course, any hopeful treasure-hunter who decides to undertake this quest, using this interpretation of the prophet's plans, would not only need to fulfill the required instructions but also the descriptive characteristics of the verses. All digging workmen please note.

Talking Dolphins?

Quand l'animal à l'homme domestique
Après grands peines et sauts viendra parler:
Le foudre à vierge sera si maléfique,
De terre prise et suspendue en l'air.

"When the animal domesticated by man after great pains and jumps will come to speak: the lightning (Sun) will be harmful to the virgin (Virgo), taken from earth and suspended in the air."

Dolphins have long been important creatures in the history of relationships between man and animals.
Above ~ a dolphin fresco from Knossos in Crete. Modern man has still apparently a lot to learn from his fellow mammals.

ERE WE FIND SOMETHING that, on the face of it, might take first prize for "weirdness." Nostradamus is telling us about an animal that mankind has domesticated: a dog, cat, horse? But he elucidates further by emphasizing the animal has suffered "great pains and leaps" before it comes to speak. For a cat to speak seems highly unlikely. On the other hand, dogs have been experimented with in terms of their ability to respond intelligently to commands and bark in a way that might conceivably indicate a real response. Dogs do jump, it is true, but not as a "pure" characteristic of their nature. One of the animals that fits this characteristic more exactly is the monkey, and monkeys have a far greater instance of intelligence than any other animal, except perhaps for one – the dolphin.

In the last decades of the 20th century dolphins have occupied our interest to a great extent because of their evident high degree of correspondence. They are very loving creatures that follow commands and requests from us in a way that others do not. They also jump, and unlike other creatures of the sea, they are mammals and could therefore be termed "animals," domesticated by man. The reference to "lightning" and the "virgin" has some astrological significance, thus giving us a timing for this change in our relationship with animals, though some interpreters have inferred that it is more likely concerned with electricity, particularly because of the last line: "...taken from earth and suspended in the air." We can infer from this that our progress with animal relations will increase towards a greater degree of correspondence in the future.

Epilogue

The following is an extract translation from the Preface written by Nostradamus to his son Cèsar.

"Events of human origin are not certain, but everything is ordered and governed by the incalculable power of God, inspiring in us not through drunken fury, nor by frantic movement, but through the influences of the stars. Only those divinely inspired can predict particular things in a prophetic spirit. For a long time I have been making many predictions, far in advance, of events that have since come to pass, naming the particular place. I attribute all this to divine power and inspiration. Pronounced events, both happy and sad, have come to pass within the "climate" of the world with increasing promptness: however, because of the possibility of harm, not just for the present but also most of the future, I became willing to remain silent and refrain from putting them into writing. Because the reigns, sects, and regions will make changes so diametrically opposite, that, if I came to reveal what will happen in the future, the great ones of the above reigns, sects, religions, and faiths would find it so badly in accord with what their fantasy wishes to hear that they would damn that which future centuries will know and see to be true. As the true Saviour said, "Give not that which is holy unto dogs, nor cast your pearls before swine, lest they trample them under their feet and turn and rend you." This has been the cause of my withholding my tongue from the populous and my pen from paper. Later, because of

the "vulgar advent" (Leoni), I decided to give way and, by obscure and perplexing sentences, tell of the causes of the future mutations of mankind, especially the most urgent ones, and the ones I saw, and in a manner that would not scandalize their delicate sentiments. All had to be written under a cloudy figure, above all things prophetic...

However, now or in the future there may be persons to whom God the Creator, through imaginative impressions, wishes to reveal some secrets of the future, in accord with judicial astrology, in much the same manner that in the past a certain power and voluntary faculty came over them like a flame, causing them to judge human and divine inspirations alike... For it is by this, together with divine inspiration and revelation, and continual watches and calculations, that we have reduced our prophecies to writing.

But what I do want to make clear to you is the judgment obtained through the calculation of the heavens. By this one has knowledge of future events while rejecting completely all imaginative things one may have. With divine and supernatural inspiration integrated with astronomical computations, one can name places and periods of time accurately, an occult property obtained through divine virtue, power, and ability. In this way, past, present, and future become but one eternity: for all things are naked and open."

Acknowledgments

Photographs, Charts & Illustrations:

Greenpeace: *Hodson,* 44; *Vennemann,* 64.

Leslie Jean-Bart Photography: 118, 158.

James Davis Travel Photography: 177, 221.

Colorific: 140; *Charlie Cole/Picture Group,* 81; *Seth Joel/Wheeler,* 93; *Dennis Brack/Black Star,* 110 120; *Richard Derk 6/87 Picture Group,* 124; *Evelyn Atwood/1990 Contact press Images:* 113; *J B Pictures/Susan Spann USA,* 115; *Tom Sobolik/Black Star,* 122; *Lawrence Manning,* 147; *Jose Vicente/Resino R/Black Star,* 168.

Images: 15, 16, 23, 24, 27, 32, 33, 35; *Coll.Chas Walker,* 10; *Stuart Kaplan/US Games Inc NY,* 135; *From Sphera Bib. Etensa, Modena,* 176.

Ancient Art & Architecture Collection: *Ronald Sheridan,* 9, 14, 18, 28, 36, 45, 68, 82, 96, 212, 217, 218, 220.

Mary Evans: 55, 71, 79, 143, 161; *Explorer/ADPC,* 13; *Paul Delaroche,* 77; *Dictionary of Gardening,* 94; *Sammes Britannia 1676,* 134; *Alonzo Chappel,* 144.

Format Photographers: *Stephanie Henry,* 30; *Brenda Prince,* 52; *Jacky Chapman,* 100; *Maggie Murray,* 201; *Meryl Levin,* 214.

Sygma: 81, 83, 126, 194; *G. Giansanti,* 41, 162; *Greg Lovett/Palm Beach Post,* 50; *Regis Bossu,* 54, 84, 108; *Paul Morse,* 47; *J. Langevin,* 66, 67, 68; *S. Compoint,* 69; *David Brauchli,* 48; *F. Darmigny,* 74; *Franco Origlia,* 189; *Antoine Gyori* 86; *R. Maiman,* 111; *Maimi Herald,* 122; *M. Elkoussy,* 145, 145; *B. Bisson,* 148, 173; *Patrick Durand,* 155; *D.Kuroda,* 78; *John Hillelson Agency,* 191; *Les Stone,* 193, 197; *Paul X Scott,* 195; *P. Le Segretain,* 207.

Salon De Provence, Maison De Nostradamus: 222.

Survival Anglia: 188.

Color Library Roses: 159.

Magnum Photos: *Susan Miselas,* 39; *David Hurn,* 42; *Eli Reed/John Hillelson Agency,* 65; *Bruno Barbey,* 70; *Abbas,* 85; *Pinkhassov,* 87, 89; *H. Kubota,* 90; *Hiroji Kubota,* 92; *Stuart Franklin,* 104; *T. Hoepker,* 109, 117; *Steve Mccurry,* 192.

Hulton Deutsch: 60, 76, 200, 203; *The Bettman Archive,* 184.

Frank Spooner Pictures: *Gamma,*128, 131.

Museum of London: 202, 202.

The Advertising Archive: *Family Planning,* 215.

Metropolitan Museum of Art: *Michael Friedsam Collection,* 73.

British Library: 7, 21.

Bruno Kortenhorst: 178.

Rex Features: *Sipa-Press,* 152.

Alpha: 204; *Dave Chancellor,* 206.

BFI Stills / Posters & Designs: 62.

Associated Press / Topham: *S Kralj/Str.,* 103.

Osho International Foundation: 57, 175, 180, 181, 182, 183.

Moonrunner / A. J. Kolpa: 55, 106, 114, 119, 132, 137, 198.

Moonrunner: 40, 127, 154, 157.

Astrology Charts:

Astro Intelligence/Astrodienst / Dr. Liz Greene / Moonrunner / A. J. Kolpa: 88, 107, 133, 136, 139, 142, 150, 151, 165, 186, 208, 210, 211.

Sources: Astrology Charts

The Astrology of America's Destiny, Vintage Books, Dane Rudhyar:
United States of America.

Mundane Astrology, Aquarian Press, 1984, M. Baigent, N. Campion & C. Harvey:
Italian Republic; United Kingdom; European Economic Community; England (Coronation of William The Conqueror).

Astrodienst Zurich:
German Democratic Republic; Opening of the Berlin Wall.

Fowler's Compendium of Nativities, Jadwiga M. Harrison:
C. G. Jung.

The Book of World Horoscopes:
Vatican City; Libya; Warsaw Pact; Switzerland ("Everlasting League").

Würtschaftliche Perspectiven Kosmische und Astrologischer Zyklen 1990 -95, Hans Gerhard Lenz:
The Swiss Franc.

Every effort has been made to trace all present copyright holders of the material in this book, whether companies or individuals. Any omission is unintentional and we will be pleased to correct any errors in future editions of this book.

Text Acknowledgments:

Page 12 – From NOSTRADAMUS AND HIS PROPHECIES by Edgar Leoni. Copyright (c) 1961 by Edgar Leoni (originally published under the title: *Nostradamus: Life and Literature*), Bell Publishing Company, New York, 1982.

Page 63 – From APOCALYPSE by D.H. Lawrence introduction Richard Aldington. Copyright 1931 by The Estate of D.H. Lawrence, renewed (c) 1959 by the Estate of Frieda Lawrence Ravagli. Used by permission of Viking Penguin, a division of Penguin Books USA Inc.

Page 65 – From BOOK OF THE HOPI by Frank Waters. Copyright (c) 1963 by Frank Waters. Used by permission of Viking Penguin, a division of Penguin Books USA Inc.